Insider Guide

Careers in Advertising and Public Relations

2005 Edition

WetFeet ®

Helping you make smarter career decisions.

WetFeet, Inc.

The Folger Building

101 Howard Street

Suite 300

San Francisco, CA 94105

Phone: (415) 284-7900 or 1-800-926-4JOB

Fax: (415) 284-7910

Website: www.wetfeet.com

Careers in Advertising and Public Relations

ISBN: 1-58207-433-X

Table of Contents

The Industries at a Glance

Opportunity Overview

- Undergrads can find account management, media, and account planning positions at ad agencies, and account management positions in PR, through on-campus recruiting or by networking.

- While most advertising creatives have BAs, you don't have to have a college degree to be a copywriter or art director, just a killer portfolio.

- Would-be PR types would also do well to put together a portfolio of work—for instance, event promotions for college organizations. Volunteering for a political campaign can also make you a stronger PR candidate.

- Internships are the best way to land a full-time job in both advertising and PR.

- Although MBAs and other advanced-degree types don't often enter advertising because entry-level jobs pay less than in other industries, their understanding of marketing can help them land a job in account management, media, or account planning.

- Most midcareer professionals looking to move into advertising or PR should be prepared to go back to square one. However, specific industry knowledge or functional expertise (e.g., in PR, lobbying experience) can start you higher up the ladder in PR. For those already in advertising or PR, it's often necessary to jump from agency to agency to move ahead.

- The severe business slump of the early 2000s caused many companies to cut advertising and other marketing spending, resulting in layoffs, office closings, and stagnant compensation in the advertising industry in particular. Already difficult to break into, advertising and PR offered even fewer opportunities in recent years than they do normally. But hiring in advertising and PR has started picking up steam, and as the economy improves and corporate America spends more on marketing and promotion, the advertising and PR job markets should improve.

Major Pluses about Careers in Advertising and PR

- Different accounts and a steady stream of new ads or press releases can mean plenty of variety.

- Advertising is one of the more relaxed industries, at least in terms of dress code and workplace formality.

- In both advertising and PR, you work with people who are smart, funny, and plugged into popular culture.

- You can change the way people think or speak. Your work might enter the national consciousness—just ask the people who were involved in the "Just Do It" ad campaign for Nike.

Major Minuses about Careers in Advertising and PR

- You may have to deal with some pretty bloated egos.

- Though you're involved in a creative effort, in the end you're not doing much for mankind. In fact, you may end up making ads for tobacco companies or writing press releases to defend corporate despoilers of the environment.

- There can be plenty of politics, both with the client and among coworkers.

- The pressure can be high and the hours long, especially before a new-business pitch or a deadline, or if the client isn't satisfied with the agency's service.

- Lack of stability—an agency might lose a big account, and suddenly 20 percent of the agency's staff is laid off.

Recruiting Overview

- Entry-level positions in account management are sometimes filled via formal campus recruiting, especially at the bigger national agencies.

- Most undergrads looking for work in advertising and PR will have to work their network of contacts.

- Aspiring copywriters and art directors get into advertising by putting together a portfolio (or *book*) of mock ads, then sending that book to different agencies' creative directors. In the past decade more and more creatives have been coming out of 2-year advertising schools, where they can create a portfolio and make connections in the industry while in school.

- Midcareer advertising and PR people looking to jump agencies will find they're judged by the success of the campaigns they've worked on.

The Industries

- Advertising and PR Overview

- Advertising: Picking and Choosing

- How the Advertising Industry Breaks Down

- Advertising Industry Trends

- Advertising Industry Rankings

- Public Relations: Picking and Choosing

- How the PR Industry Breaks Down

- Public Relations Industry Trends

Advertising and PR Overview

Maybe you're an English major whose friends are all receiving job offers from consulting firms, banks, and the like, and you're wondering just what the heck the business world has to offer you. Maybe you're a banker, but frustrated because your job doesn't let you express creativity or take advantage of your abiding interest in popular culture and the media. Maybe you're a struggling writer or artist who's tired of living on ramen and happy-hour buffets, and you've come to the conclusion that a cell phone and a steady paycheck don't necessarily make a person a sellout. Then you turn on the television or pick up a newspaper or magazine, and suddenly it hits you: Why not work in advertising or PR?

Advertising

In broad terms, an advertising agency is a marketing consultant. It helps the client (a manufacturer of consumer products like Nike, perhaps, or a service-oriented company like Charles Schwab & Co.) with all aspects of its marketing efforts—everything from strategy to concept to execution. Strategy involves helping the client make high-level business decisions, such as what new products the client should develop or how the client should define or "brand" itself to the world. Concept is where the agency takes the client's strategy and turns it into specific ideas for advertisements—such as a series of ads featuring extreme athletes for a soft-drink maker whose strategy is to make inroads in the teen market. Execution is where the agency turns the concept into reality with the production of the actual ads: the print layout, the film shoot, the audio taping. Full-service agencies also handle the placement of the ads in newspapers, magazines, radio, and so on, so that they reach their intended audience. Sometimes the agency works in conjunction with the client's marketing department; other times—when the client doesn't have a marketing department—the agency takes on that role.

Public Relations

Unlike advertising, PR involves communicating an organization's message to the press, rather than directly to the target market. In other words, where advertising is paid media exposure, PR results in free media exposure. The objective in PR is to use the press to reach the target market because, when mediated by a supposedly objective third party, the message becomes more credible and thus more powerful. The goal in PR is to make your client (or your company, if you work in-house in a corporate communications or marketing communications position) look great. To do this, PR professionals primarily work with the members of the press to get stories that reflect positively on their clients' products or images in newspapers and magazines, on the radio, or on TV. PR professionals might also speak on behalf of client organizations; arrange for clients' presence at appropriate industry events; help mitigate harmful publicity when, for instance, the federal government sues a client for antitrust violations; or help clients come up with an overall marketing strategy for, say, a new product launch. PR professionals work for everyone from big companies to government agencies to charitable organizations to famous individuals—anyone with a public image (or an important message or a saleable product) that can benefit from PR expertise.

Outlook

The advertising and PR industries were hit hard by the decline of the dot coms, the tech downturn, and the overall recession. Remember all those expensive dot-com Super Bowl ads from a few years back? A lot of those companies are no longer in business—and, like their more traditional brick-and-mortar Corporate America cousins, those that have survived are much less willing to plunk down millions of dollars on advertising or PR. But companies are starting to spend again, albeit not at the levels of the late 1990s. Whereas U.S. advertising industry revenue was up just 0.6 percent in 2001, in 2003 it rose by nearly 4 percent. The situation in PR has been similar. For a few years, many advertising and PR agencies were forced to lay off employees, close offices, and cut or freeze salaries. Fortunately for those in the industry (and those looking to get into it), things are looking up; as advertising and PR spending increases, agencies are finally beginning to add a trickle of new jobs. As one insider says, "It's not a great time in the history of advertising to get employment, but the employment climate does seem to be picking up."

You'll face stiff competition if you want a career in advertising or PR. Still, these remain attractive industries to many job seekers. In advertising, many writers and artists are drawn to agencies' creative and production departments because the salaries are much higher in the ad game than in the starving artist game. For business types, advertising offers an exciting proximity to the creative process, if not an actual role in that process. PR offers liberal arts types jobs that can be steady and fairly lucrative while still being creative. Pros in both industries often enjoy perks like dinners, plays, and ballgames with clients. And everyone in these industries gets to spend their days with the hippest, most culturally aware coworkers around—and play a role in shaping the stories and advertisements that shape our culture.

The Bottom Line

All those English and art history majors (and other liberal arts majors) you went to school with? It's pretty likely that a fair-sized chunk of them are just like you—interested in advertising and PR, because these industries offer "real" jobs to creative people like English and art history majors.

It's exceedingly difficult to start in these industries in anything but an entry-level position, and there's a lot of competition for relatively few low-paying jobs. As a result, if you want to work in advertising or PR, be prepared to start at the bottom and work your contacts to get interviews. Although some of the bigger agencies do recruit on campus for entry-level hires (particularly in advertising account management), most entry-level hires are not recruited. The best way to get a foot in the door in these industries is through internships.

In advertising, the easiest routes into the marketing and business side of the business are entry-level media positions and administrative assistant positions. They don't pay that well and they involve lots of grunt work, but you'll get a chance to show your stuff and get promoted. If you're a creative, you can't get a job in advertising without a book of your work. For entry-level copywriting or art-direction positions, this means designing and producing mock advertisements.

In PR, you'll probably start as an account coordinator or, if you go into communications at a company, a PR coordinator. These, too, are entry-level positions that involve lots of grunt work. Be prepared to prove that you have excellent writing and communication skills to get in the door in PR.

Advertising: Picking and Choosing

If you're considering going into advertising, it's important to spend some time thinking about the kind of advertising agency you'd like to work for. Just as there are many different kinds of ads—print, radio, television, outdoor, banner— there are many different kinds of ad agencies. Two factors to consider when thinking about what type of agency you'd fit best with are location and whether the agency is creative- or account-driven.

Location

Location is important because it determines whether you'll be part of a sizable network of advertising people. It also goes a long way toward determining the quality of the accounts you will work on and the respect you'll get from your peers. Unless you work for a Fallon or a Wieden + Kennedy, you'll find you need to work in New York, Los Angeles, Chicago, or San Francisco to be at the pinnacle of the ad game. Of those, New York has the biggest and strongest advertising community.

Location is also important because many advertising markets, especially smaller ones, are less diversified, more reliant on revenues from a single industry, than are big markets like that in New York. If a smaller market's key industry or industries are going well, then those markets will have plenty of advertising work—but if the industry or industries are performing poorly, then the local advertising industry can take a major hit. For example, in the past few years, the advertising industry in San Francisco has been decimated, as hundreds of dot coms folded and bigger tech companies saw poor financial results.

Creative versus Account-Driven

It's also important to decide whether you're more interested in working for a creative agency or an account-driven agency and to do some research to learn which agencies fit those descriptions. The biggest difference between account-driven and creative agencies is that account-driven agencies' ads usually focus on product benefits, while creative agencies' ads focus on brand image. As a result, account-driven agencies end up with accounts like Crispix, a cereal brand built around the product's crispiness in milk. Creative agencies end up with accounts where lifestyle or image is more important, such as Sega, which uses in-your-face advertising to connect with its teen target market.

At account-driven agencies, a premium is placed on smart strategic thinking, and all advertising is judged, internally and by the client, on how well it executes the client's strategy. Account services people generally drive the strategy process at these agencies. At creative agencies the emphasis is more on the creative product and on coming up with concepts that are new, funny, wild, or unusual. The creative department is more in the driver's seat in determining strategy and is more likely to dictate to the client what the advertising will look like. While both types of agencies do market testing to help determine the strategy and the content of the ads, the creative agency is more likely to move ahead with an ad that intuition says is great but testing says is weak.

How the Advertising Industry Breaks Down

While location and creative philosophy are important factors in judging agencies, they are by no means the only factors. Though the following breakdown of the industry is somewhat arbitrary and certainly incomplete, it should give you a good idea of the variety of opportunities available.

Traditional Agencies

Traditional agencies handle a variety of account types—everything from packaged goods to sporting goods to automobiles to computer software. They are also full-service agencies, meaning they offer all the services related to the strategy, concept, and execution of advertising. (Increasingly, the full-service concept includes marketing services such as public relations, direct mail, and interactive.) Traditional agencies can be further broken down by size, as follows.

Big Global Networks

In the past decade, global has become the way to go. Several huge global marketing and media conglomerates now dominate the advertising industry. These include Omnicom Group, WPP Group, the Interpublic Group, Havas, and Publicis Groupe. They are joined by advertising agencies that have expanded their operations by opening offices around the world and by acquiring other marketing and media companies. Together, these firms own many of the major players in traditional and interactive advertising. Publicis Groupe, for example, owns Publicis Worldwide, Saatchi & Saatchi, and Leo Burnett Worldwide.

In the old days, being big meant being corporate and account-driven. Though that's still often the case, it's not the rule it once was. One reason is that advertising has changed, with many advertisers now recognizing the value of catchy creative work. Another is that big companies now own what were until recently independent shops known for strong creative. Omnicom, for instance, owns Goodby, Silverstein, and Interpublic owns Lowe & Partners.

Smaller Shops

Although a lot of hot shops have been snatched up by the big global holding companies, there are still plenty of smaller shops—some with as few as five employees. Often these are creative boutiques—agencies started by people from bigger agencies who have hung out their own shingle in order to follow their vision of what makes good advertising.

At smaller agencies, the boundaries between different departments are often not as pronounced as at larger agencies. While the staff at bigger agencies is divided by client, in a smaller agency people often work on several accounts at once. Mad Dogs & Englishmen in New York and Butler, Shine, Stern, and Partners in Sausalito, CA, are two of the hundreds of smaller shops.

Specialty Agencies

Some agencies focus on certain segments of the advertising business. Following are several of the different kinds of specialty shops.

Interactive Agencies

Interactive agencies specialize in online marketing and advertising. This includes everything from concepting, designing, and placing banner ads to designing corporate websites to developing e-commerce solutions for corporations. This segment of the industry was devastated in the early 2000s, when dot coms, which spent a lot of money as a group on online advertising, started collapsing left and right. But the segment looks to be on the rebound, as advertisers from a broad range of industries try out new online strategies with a more realistic perspective on what advertising on the Internet can and cannot do.

Direct Marketing Agencies

While many full-service agencies have direct marketing units, there are also many independent direct marketing companies. These agencies specialize in designing and distributing direct mail—better known as *junk mail*.

Ethnic Agencies

Ethnic agencies focus on marketing to ethnic-minority markets. Their clients include makers of products—such as certain foods or hair-care products—targeted at specific ethnic markets. Ethnic agencies also may be hired by makers of more general products to increase visibility and market share among certain minority audiences. For example, McDonald's may hire an ethnic agency to do advertising aimed specifically at African-Americans. Players include Burrell Communications, Dieste Harmel & Partners, and Muse Cordero Chen. While many other segments of the advertising industry have struggled of late, ethnic shops have been growing due to the changing awareness of demographics in the United States. Indeed, in 2003, Hispanic agencies in the United States grew by an average of almost 14 percent.

Automotive Agencies

While many of the big general advertising agencies handle automotive accounts, a number of smaller agencies focus on automotive work, such as Doner. Clients sometimes divide their branding and product-benefit advertising between nationally renowned general agencies and automotive agencies.

Health Care Agencies

The legal requirements shaping health care advertising have made this a specialty field within the industry. The work can include creating promotional and educational materials in addition to producing traditional ads. Very few accounts buy TV time. Players here include Cline Davis & Mann, Klemtner Advertising, and Sudler & Hennessy. This segment of the industry is growing faster than most other segments; indeed, the health care advertising market grew by nearly 7 percent in 2003.

In-House Agencies

Some corporations create and produce some or all of their own advertising. For example, Charles Schwab & Co. and MasterCard both have in-house ad departments. Usually, these are more corporate in feel and produce advertising that's not as exciting as that of general agencies.

Advertising Industry Trends

Consolidation

Like so many other industries, advertising has experienced lots of consolidation in recent years, as companies join forces to lower costs and stay competitive in the global marketplace. In advertising, bigger size means more clout with media outlets and, thus, lower advertising costs and more PR pitch phone calls answered by news editors. This trend is also a result of the fact that by owning several different advertising or PR agencies, a single holding company can control several competing accounts without conflict of interest.

Account Planning

Account planning—also known as *strategic planning*—was developed in English ad agencies in the 1960s and 1970s. It took a while, but in recent years the American advertising industry has discovered account planning in a big way. Account planning is a discipline that aims to increase understanding of the consumer. Today, account planning is such an integral part of many American ad agencies that it's the account planners who do most of the strategizing on behalf of clients, rather than the account management staff.

Interactive Advertising

"It's baaaaack!" Like a B-movie monster, interactive advertising has roared back onto the scene, once again a viable business. Interactive advertising, which was brand spanking new just 10 years ago, has finally been around long enough to understand what advertising works on the Web, and what doesn't. And while the interactive advertising market collapsed when the dot-com bubble burst and most Internet start-ups (which happened to do the bulk of online advertising) went out of business, in recent times companies have once again begun buying online advertising. And interactive agency performance has improved tremendously: In 2003, interactive agencies grew by an average of nearly 21 percent.

Other New Media

The Internet is not the only new medium when it comes to advertising. It seems that people are jaded by the overload of ads in traditional media, such as TV and newspapers, and often don't even pay attention to ads. As a result, for years, now, advertisers have been trying to get your attention through nontraditional advertising media such as the movies, where product placement has become a permanent part of business or on the marquees of professional sports venues (e.g., San Francisco's SBC Park or Los Angeles' Staples Center). And, thanks to Channel One, advertising has been a part of daily life in many schools in the United States.

Other nifty places where you can now see ads include bus rooftops (ads atop buses reach the professional market that works in office towers, apparently) and the bottom of golf holes. Beer ads have begun to show up on disinfectant cakes in men's room urinals. One company has been trying to get ads on police cars. And many cities and towns have even accepted corporate money that allows their benefactors to be their "sponsors"; even New York is moving forward with plans to be "sponsored" by Snapple.

O, Canada

In an effort to lower production costs, and especially in response to the slump in advertising billings in recent years, more and more TV commercials are being shot in Canada. (Especially in Toronto and Vancouver, both of which have well-developed facilities and labor pools for commercial production.)

Advertising Industry Rankings

These are the biggest advertising agencies headquartered in the United States, by 2003 U.S. revenue, minus specialty and subsidiary agencies.

Top U.S. Advertising Agencies, by 2003 U.S. Advertising Revenue

Agency	Headquarters	Revenue ($M)	1-Yr. Change (%)
J. Walter Thompson Co.	New York	456	16
Leo Burnett Worldwide	Chicago	404	7
McCann Erickson Worldwide	New York	300	0
BBDO Worldwide	New York	279	11
Grey Worldwide	New York	271	15
DDB Worldwide Communications	New York	252	7
Ogilvy & Mather Worldwide	New York	236	18
Foote Cone & Belding Worldwide	New York	222	1
Y&R Advertising	New York	216	13
Publicis Worldwide	New York	201	12
Saatchi & Saatchi	New York	196	11
Euro RSCG Worldwide	New York	194	1
Deutsch	New York	167	6
Arnold Worldwide	Boston	150	−7
Campbell-Ewald	Warren, MI	146	−3
Lowe & Partners Worldwide	New York	134	−7
TBWA Worldwide	New York	126	10
Doner	Southfield, MI	123	12
Richards Group	Dallas	115	11
Hill, Holliday, Connors, Cosmopulos	Boston	103	2
Campbell Mithun	Minneapolis	96	0
RPA	Santa Monica, CA	93	1
Dailey & Associates	West Hollywood, CA	89	−1
Zimmerman & Partners	Ft. Lauderdale, FL	86	7
Fallon Worldwide	Minneapolis	82	11

Source: www.AdAge.com.

Public Relations: Picking and Choosing

In terms of numbers of PR jobs, you're far more likely to make a PR career for yourself at a big agency like Burson-Marsteller or Porter Novelli, which employ thousands of people. However, by far, most PR agencies are tiny in comparison, with just ten or 12 employees. This means that, while you're far more likely to find work in PR in New York, Chicago, Washington, San Francisco, or other major metropolitan areas, there are always opportunities in other parts of the country. But, of course, you'll have to work harder (read: network) to learn about those opportunities. And even if you do want to work at a small agency, you'll probably be best off starting at a big agency, where entry-level hires are the norm and not the exception, and you can get the experience that smaller shops often require of candidates.

How the PR Industry Breaks Down

Full-Service Agencies

Most of the PR agencies in this category are part of big, global marketing networks. For instance, Burson-Marsteller, Hill and Knowlton, and Ogilvy Public Relations are all part of WPP. Edelman is pretty much the only huge PR agency that remains independent. While these and other agencies are often known for expertise in particular areas of PR, in general they offer a full range of PR services, everything from media relations to deep knowledge of a variety of industries and an ability to provide extensive strategy assistance to clients.

This category is not limited to behemoth agencies, though. Many smaller shops provide whatever PR services their clients need. The difference is that smaller agencies' clients are usually smaller, with less sophisticated needs—and due to limited resources, smaller full-service agencies usually don't have the clout in terms of making a PR splash that their bigger cousins do.

Specialized Agencies

Some agencies specialize in public relations for clients in a specific industry or industries or specialize in a specific public relations function or functions. For instance, Brodeur Worldwide and Text 100 specialize in technology, whereas Alan Taylor Communications and Matlock Advertising & PR specialize in sports marketing and multicultural PR, respectively. Agencies in this category are generally smaller than big full-service agencies, and it can be necessary to start in a bigger organization to get hired into them.

In-House Public Relations

Most big companies have in-house communications departments. These can be responsible for some of the same areas covered by PR agencies, such as corporate communications, employee communications, or consumer marketing. In bigger organizations, they can also act as full-service, in-house PR agencies, which handle most of the day-to-day PR chores for the company. They might also work with outside PR agencies on bigger campaigns or on specialized PR challenges, such as litigation consulting or crisis PR.

Public Relations Industry Trends

Consolidation

Like the advertising industry, the PR industry has been marked by extensive consolidation over the past decade or so. As in advertising, in PR bigger size means more clout with media outlets. And a single holding company can control several competing PR accounts without conflict of interest. In general, ad and PR agencies that exist under mammoth holding companies (WPP, Omnicom, etc.) operate as stand-alone businesses, but there can be cases where business synergies result from the new ties between agencies. For instance, if you go into PR you may end up trying to place stories about an ad campaign created by an ad agency owned by the same holding company your agency is owned by.

The Internet

The Internet has changed the face of PR. On the one hand, it offers a wealth of opportunities to get the word out on behalf of your client. And PR professionals can reach specific audiences as never before, by targeting industry- or interest-specific news sites, message boards, and weblogs.

The flip side of the coin is that it's now harder than ever to manage the release of information. Online news sites are updated 24/7, meaning the only PR professional who's truly on top of managing the news about his or her client is the PR professional who never sleeps. And the interactive nature of the Internet means that negative news about your client can pop up at any time, anywhere from a popular blog to a high-traffic message board.

Training

The PR industry has been notoriously lacking in terms of training for young professionals. In many agencies, most new employees still suffer through a sink-or-swim, learn-as-you-go period early in their careers. However, many agencies are beginning to recognize the benefits of offering formal training—to orient new employees, to ensure that valuable knowledge is available across the agency, and to help retain valuable employees. Hill and Knowlton, for instance, now offers a Virtual Academy, which provides online training programs.

The Advertising Agencies

- The Top Agencies

- Other Agencies

The Top Agencies

Following are profiles of 20 top advertising agencies in the United States.

Arnold Worldwide Partners

101 Huntington Avenue
Boston, MA 02199
Phone: 617-587-8000
Fax: 617-587-8008
www.arnoldworldwide.com

Key Financial Facts

2003 U.S. advertising revenue: $194 million
1-yr. growth rate: –5 percent

Personnel Highlights

Number of employees: 1,800 (est.)
1-yr. growth rate: 20 percent (est.)

Key Facts

- Second at the 2003 One Show in terms of number of Pencil awards received, with a total of nine, for creative for Volkswagen and the American Legacy Foundation.
- Received an overall grade of C in the 2003 *Adweek* Agency Report Cards.
- Clients include Volkswagen, Royal Caribbean, and Titleist.

Overview

Things haven't been easy for Arnold Worldwide lately. Like many other agencies, Arnold, which is owned by Havas, has suffered layoffs in recent years: In 2003, it laid off 15 percent of staff at its McLean, VA, office, and 5 percent in Boston. In 2002, longtime CEO Pat McGrath retired, Arnold closed its San Francisco office due to soft business, and the agency lost accounts such as Procter & Gamble's Bounty and Era and ExxonMobil. In 2003, the agency added Amtrak and Pergo, but lost Welch's, White Wave's Silk Soymilk, and Monster.com, as well as failing in pitches for several Pfizer medications, Nextel, Jergens, Polaroid, Cotton Inc., Nikon, and FEMA—as well as losing a couple of top executives in the New York office.

Recent compelling work from Arnold includes antismoking ads for the American Legacy Foundation and ads for the VW Touareg SUV and Beetle convertible.

Havas had been looking to Arnold as a global creative network, but has decided that that plan isn't working out. As a result, its network of 25 offices in six countries is being disassembled, making Arnold once again a U.S.-focused agency. It hopes to find more success now that it's operating on a smaller scale once again.

BBDO Worldwide

1285 Avenue of the Americas

New York, NY 10019

Phone: 212-459-5000

Fax: 212-459-6645

www.bbdo.com

Key Financial Facts

2003 U.S. advertising revenue: $495 million

1-yr. growth rate: 10 percent

Personnel Highlights

Not available.

Key Facts

- Owned by the Omnicom Group.
- Clients include Pepsi, Pizza Hut, FedEx, Cingular, Gillette, Hormel, Frito-Lay, and GE.
- Detroit office cut 100 jobs in May 2004.

Overview

BBDO, which is a subsidiary of advertising holding company Omnicom, was formed in 1917 when George Batten's agency merged with Barton, Durstine & Osborn. Throughout its history BBDO has built a reputation for strong creative work. In the middle of the 20th century, it came up with Dupont's "Better things through better living through chemistry" slogan; in 1972, it launched the "Have it your way" Burger King campaign.

More recently, notable work from BBDO includes Visa ads featuring Derek Jeter and George Steinbrenner and a DaimlerChrysler ad in which a man rejoices at inheriting empty swampland because it gives him a playground in which he can drive his Jeep Grand Cherokee as long and as hard as he likes.

Recent wins include the $150 million AOL account, the Lubriderm account, the Jim Beam account, and the Aquafina account. Overall, the agency won six of 14 pitches. However, it lost the KFC and Caress accounts. Also, in 2003 clients including Chrysler, Cingular, and GE increased spending, but Pepsi, Wrigley, and Office Depot cut spending.

DDB Worldwide Communications Group Inc.

437 Madison Avenue
New York, NY 10022
Phone: 212-415-2000
Fax: 212-415-3414
www.ddb.com

Key Financial Facts

2003 U.S. advertising revenue: $430 million
1-yr. growth rate: 4 percent

Personnel Highlights

Number of employees: 13,000 (est.)
1-yr. growth rate: not available

Key Facts

- Owned by the Omnicom Group.
- Named the 2004 Global Agency of the Year by *Advertising Age*.

Overview

DDB Worldwide, a subsidiary of Omnicom, has a long history of creative excellence. It was responsible for the "Mama mia, that's a spicy meatball" ad for Alka-Seltzer and the 1970s "Mikey likes it!" ads for Life cereal. After scoring with the "Whassup?" Budweiser campaign in 2000, it has followed up with the Budweiser "True" campaign.

In 2003 the agency won new business from clients including Philips Electronics, Lipton, Novartis' Consumer Health division, Home Depot, and the Illinois and Texas lotteries. It also won $60 million in new Hershey's business. DDB lost its Qwest, Starwood Hotels & Resorts, and Hamilton Beach/Procter Silex accounts.

The agency has made some key creative hires in recent times, in an attempt to return to the top creative ranks in the industry.

DDB, named after founders Ned Doyle, Maxwell Dane, and Bill Bernbach, opened shop in 1949. Today the DDB network consists of some 200 offices around the world.

Deutsch, Inc.

111 Eighth Avenue
14th Floor
New York, NY 10011
Phone: 212-981-7600
Fax: 212-981-7525
www.deutschinc.com

Key Financial Facts

2003 U.S. advertising revenue: $312 million
1-yr. growth rate: 15 percent

Personnel Highlights

Number of employees: 1,024
1-yr. growth rate: 1.3 percent

Key Facts

- Owned by the Interpublic Group of Companies.
- Received an overall grade of A– in the 2003 *Adweek* Agency Report Cards.
- Clients include Bank of America, Coors Light, Tommy Hilfiger, Snapple, Real California Cheese, Monster, and Expedia.com.

Overview

Founded as a print-focused boutique ad agency in 1969, Deutsch is now a major player in the industry. Long considered too small and creatively aggressive to be a real force in the industry, in the past decade it has transformed into a big agency. Today, CEO Donny Deutsch (son of founder David Deutsch) spends more time working on his cable news-channel show, The Big Idea with Donny Deutsch, than he does on running the agency. But that doesn't seem to matter much, as revenue grows year after year (indeed, Deutsch has seen double-digit revenue growth in each of the past 7 years), and the agency continues to produce notable work such as the Coors Light "Wingman" ads, the California Milk Advisory Board's ads featuring talking cows, and the "Today's the day" campaign for Monster.

Wins in 2003 included Bank of America, T.G.I. Friday's, Monster, Johnson & Johnson's Tylenol and St. Joseph's, and Novartis. Losses included Burger King and MCI work. The agency also resigned the Pfizer account after the client demanded that Deutsch reveal executive salaries and other financial information. These days, it's bracing itself for the potential loss of Mitsubishi business, as that client suffers slumping sales and possible overhaul at the executive level.

The agency has offices in Chicago, Los Angeles, and New York. In addition to advertising, it does direct marketing and PR.

Fallon Worldwide

50 S. 6th Street, Ste. 2800
Minneapolis, MN 55402
Phone: 612-758-2345
Fax: 612-758-2346
www.fallon.com

Key Facts

2003 U.S. advertising revenue: $98 million
1-yr. growth rate: 20 percent

Personnel Highlights

Number of employees (2002): 464
1-yr. growth rate: 5.5 percent

Key Facts

- Part of the Publicis Groupe.
- Took home three Pencil awards from the 2003 One Show, for creative for BMW and Finnegans.
- Received an overall grade of A– in the 2003 *Adweek* Agency Report Cards.
- The "Lip-synch" campaign for Citi: Identity Theft was named the 2003 *Adweek* Campaign of the Year.

Overview

Fallon Worldwide, formerly Fallon McElligott, was acquired by the Publicis Groupe in 2001. The agency has offices in Minneapolis, New York, London, Singapore, Hong Kong, and Sao Paulo. At one time a regional agency, like Weiden + Kennedy, Fallon showed the world in the 1980s that there's advertising excellence outside of New York.

The agency has suffered no major account losses of late, while winning a major account in Subway, as well as winning work from the Bahamas Ministry of Tourism and Virgin Mobile. Existing clients, such as BMW, Citibank, and United Airlines, also increased spending in 2003.

Notable work of late includes its campaign for Citibank, featuring crime victims dubbed with the voices of thieves who've stolen their identities and ripped them off (*Adweek*'s campaign of the year).

The agency added a seventh international member to its network by acquiring Gram Advertising in Tokyo in 2003.

Foote, Cone & Belding Worldwide

150 E. 42nd Street

New York, NY 10017

Phone: 212-885-3000

Fax: 212-885-2803

www.fcb.com

Key Financial Facts

2003 U.S. advertising revenue: $350 million

1-yr. growth rate: 0 percent

Personnel Highlights

Not available.

Key Facts

- Owned by the Interpublic Group of Companies.
- Received an overall grade of C– in the 2003 *Adweek* Agency Report Cards.
- Clients include SC Johnson, Taco Bell, Qwest, KFC, Kraft, Mattel, Merck, Coors, and Archer Daniels Midland.

Overview

Foote, Cone & Belding Worldwide, which was founded in 1873 and is the world's third-oldest ad agency, operates U.S. offices in Chicago, New York, San Francisco, Seattle, and Irvine, CA. FCB San Francisco, known for excellence in creative (it has created campaigns such as the California Raisins), has been hard hit by the tech decline—and overall, the agency hasn't been doing as well as other top agencies.

The good news in 2003 was the win of the $280 million KFC account, along with the wins of GlaxoSmithKline's Valtrex and the Auto Club of Southern California, as well as additional work for clients Hewlett-Packard, Levi's, and

Kraft's Back to Nature. Losses included JP Morgan Chase retail, and clients including Levi's, Kraft, Hilton Hotels, and Samsung cut spending. Creative coming out of FCB offices of late has not been noteworthy. Management turnover seems to have slowed, though, and the agency is hoping that some stability along those lines will result in a return to past levels of glory.

The FCB network comprises some 200 offices around the world.

Goodby, Silverstein & Partners

720 California Street

San Francisco, CA 94108

Phone: 415-392-0669

Fax: 415-788-4303

www.goodbysilverstein.com

Key Financial Facts

2003 U.S. advertising revenue: $75 million

1-yr. growth rate: 7 percent

Personnel Highlights

Number of employees (2002): 400 (est.)

1-yr. growth rate: 109.4 percent (est.)

Key Facts

- Owned by the Omnicom Group.

- Jeff Goodby and Rich Silverstein were inducted into the One Club Creative Hall of Fame in 2004, joining the likes of Bill Bernbach, David Ogilvy, and Leo Burnett.

- Goodby doesn't just do TV, radio, and print. The agency was at the head of the class at the 2004 One Show Interactive Awards.

Overview

A subsidiary of advertising giant Omnicom, Goodby is a relative newcomer to the advertising game, but it has earned a major reputation for creative excellence in its fewer than 20 years of existence through such work as the "Got Milk?" and the "Louie the Lizard" Budweiser campaigns.

Wins in 2003 included AT&T Wireless, Banana Republic, and Emerald Nuts; in addition, existing client eBay boosted spending. Downsides include a decrease in spending from Goodyear Tire & Rubber and the loss of clients such as SBC Communications, E-Trade, and Match.com. The big bummer here is that due to the client's pending merger with Cingular, the shop will no longer have the AT&T Wireless account.

Recent notable work includes an ad for Hewlett-Packard that features Renaissance paintings coming to life in The National Gallery in London; eBay spots featuring lavish, impromptu renderings of show tunes; and a Budweiser ad depicting a bored boyfriend hearing a baseball play-by-play coming from his girlfriend's mouth, when in fact she's talking about emotions.

Grey Worldwide

777 Third Avenue

New York, NY 10017

Phone: 212-546-2000

Fax: 212-546-1495

www.grey.com

Key Financial Facts

2003 U.S. advertising revenue: $510 million

1-yr. growth rate: 20 percent

Personnel Highlights

Not available.

Key Facts

- Part of the Grey Global Group, one of the giant media corporations that own most major advertising and media agencies these days.
- Did the advertising for the worldwide launch of Nokia's N-Gage brand, an account worth $100 million.

Overview

Grey, the crown jewel of the Grey Global Group, is one of the giants of the advertising industry. The agency was formed in 1917 and went public in 1965. Grey is known for its marketing and branding expertise and its account-driven philosophy. It likes to think of itself as more a marketing consultant than an advertising agency. To this end, Grey counts media, research, and public relations among its strengths. The result has been some very long relationships with clients, including Procter & Gamble, which has been a client for more than 40 years.

In 2003, the agency had the top revenue-to-staff ratio among national agencies. Wins included the big Kmart account, Wells Fargo, BMW Western dealers,

Veritas, and Diet Coke with Lime, and existing clients including Aetna, BellSouth, Oracle, and Procter & Gamble upped spending. The agency resigned Health Choice, and its only significant outright loss was the $20 million Orville Redenbacher account.

Grey operates in some 90 countries around the world.

GSD&M Advertising

828 W. 6th Street

Austin, TX 78703

Phone: 512-427-4736

Fax: 512-427-4700

www.gsdm.com

Key Financial Facts

2003 U.S. advertising revenue: $100 million

1-yr. growth rate: 11 percent

Personnel Highlights

Number of employees (2002): 565

1-yr. growth rate: 5.8 percent

Key Facts

- Owned by the Omnicom Group.

- Clients include Chili's, Charles Schwab, Dial Corp., DreamWorks, Kinko's, Land Rover, Mastercard, Pennzoil, the PGA Tour, SBC, Southwest, the Houston Rockets, the U.S. Air Force, and Wal-Mart.

Overview

GSD&M, which is owned by Omnicom Group, was founded in 1971 by six graduates of the University of Texas. In 2003 the agency's wins included SBC residential creative, Tostitos, smoking-cessation work for the American Legacy Foundation, image work for the U.S. Olympic Committee, and on-air promotion for CBS Sports. In addition, existing clients MasterCard and Brinker International upped spending. But Kinko's cut its spending drastically, Dreamworks SKG and Dial also cut spending, and the agency lost its $15 million Shell chemicals account.

Notable recent work includes the "Wanna get away?" campaign for Southwest Airlines, featuring people in embarrassing situations they'd love to escape, and a CBS Sports ad featuring a golf commentator whispering his food order at a fast-food drive-through window.

The agency has started moving down an exciting new path with its Imax film production about Texas. In 2004, the agency began production on another film. Areas of emphasis for the near future include landing a carmaker client and strengthening the media unit so it can better compete against giant media companies.

These days, GSD&M, which counts Krispy Kreme among its key clients, must be hoping that the low-carb diet craze does not crush demand for donuts.

J. Walter Thompson Company

466 Lexington Avenue

New York, NY 10017

Phone: 212-210-7000

Fax: 212-210-7770

www.jwt.com

Key Financial Facts

2003 U.S. advertising revenue: $513 million

1-yr. growth rate: 5 percent

Personnel Highlights

Number of employees: 8,500

1-yr. growth rate: –7.6 percent

Key Facts

- Owned by the WPP Group.

- Operates in 150 cities in 86 countries.

Overview

JWT began in 1864 as Carlton & Smith in New York. In 1879 James Walter Thompson bought the agency from his boss for $500. In 1887 JWT became the first agency to actually write advertisements; previously, agencies arranged for the placement of ads in the media, and clients wrote the ads. It became the first full-service agency in 1895, offering ad layout, package design, and logo design services. (Among the agency's famous logo designs: the Rock of Gibraltar for Prudential Insurance.) In 1987 the agency was acquired by the media holding company WPP Group.

When JWT's parent, the WPP Group, disbanded the Bates Worldwide advertising agency in 2003, JWT inherited Bates' Pfizer and T. Rowe Price accounts. (The Pfizer account was worth $200 million.) Wins included Unilever's Caress, FEMA, and McLeodUSA. Losses included Unilever's Lubriderm, Pfizer's Celebrex, Sun Microsystems, and Miller's MGD and Foster's brands. The agency also won the $40 million Office Max account, but then lost it within 6 months.

JWT's New York office absorbed some 150 Bates employees, and Bates' London office was folded into JWT's London office.

The JWT network contains some 300 offices around the world.

Leo Burnett Worldwide, Inc.

35 W. Wacker Drive
Chicago, IL 60601
Phone: 312-220-5959
Fax: 312-220-3299
www.leoburnett.com

Key Financial Facts

2003 U.S. advertising revenue: $315 million
1-yr. growth rate: 5 percent

Personnel Highlights

Not available.

Key Facts

- Owned by the Publicis Groupe.
- Has had Kellogg's, Philip Morris, and Procter & Gamble as clients for more than 50 years. Other clients include Visa, McDonald's, Kraft Foods, Hallmark, Morgan Stanley, and Walt Disney.

Overview

Leo Burnett, which is much more an account-driven agency than a creative shop, is one of the giants of the American advertising scene. The agency was founded in 1935 in Chicago. Among its famous creations are the Jolly Green Giant, Morris the Cat, and the Marlboro Man, as well as taglines such as "Fly the friendly skies" and "Tastes great. Less filling."

Account wins in 2003 included Gateway, ConAgra's Healthy Choice, and Chef Boyardee. The agency also took on the $250 million Philips account when its parent Publicis shuttered D'Arcy Masius Benton & Bowles. Losses included Delta and Sara Lee's Ball Park and Jimmy Dean brands. Recent notable work includes the "Army of One" campaign for the U.S. Army and Allstate ads featuring the actor who plays the U.S. president on the TV show *24*.

The Leo Burnett network contains nearly 100 offices in some 80 countries around the globe. The shop is moving through a period of change these days as it adapts to new ownership.

Lowe & Partners Worldwide

Headquarters:

Bowater House, 68-114

Knightsbridge

London

SW1X 7LT, United Kingdom

Phone: 44-20-7894-5033

U.S. Headquarters:

150 E. 42nd Street

New York, NY 10017

Phone: 212-605-8000

Fax: 212-605-5656

www.loweworldwide.com

Key Financial Facts

2003 U.S. advertising revenue: $217 million

1-yr. growth rate: 6 percent

Personnel Highlights

Number of employees (2002): 8,850 (est.)

1-yr. growth rate: not available

Key Facts

- Owned by the Interpublic Group of Companies.
- Clients include Johnson & Johnson, Saab, Unilever, Nestle, Coca-Cola, and General Motors.
- More than 180 offices in more than 80 countries.

Overview

Lowe traces its history back to 1981, when Sir Frank Lowe and six colleagues created Lowe Howard-Spink in London. By 1985 the agency, now called Lowe Howard-Spink Marschalk, had won the *AdAge* International Agency of the Year award. Around the same time, the agency began assembling a network of like-minded creative agencies. In 1999 the Lowe network merged with Ammirati

Puris Lintas, to become Lowe Lintas and Partners. In 2002, the agency changed its name again, to its current name.

In 2003, the agency merged with fellow Interpublic shop Bozell, thus taking on accounts such as Verizon Wireless and Milk PEP/Milk DMI. (Lowe promptly proceeded to lose Verizon in mid-review.) Additional wins in 2003 included Macy's, Carfax, and global Electrolux. Losses included Valvoline and Hellmann's for Unilever Bestfoods. Creatively, Lowe is known for excellence, but recently the network's performance has been mixed.

Lowe is a top ten global agency, but whether it can survive in that incarnation in the current atmosphere of industry consolidation remains to be seen.

In North America, Lowe has offices in New York, Chicago, and Toronto.

McCann Worldgroup

622 Third Avenue
New York, NY 10017
Phone: 646-865-2000
Fax: 646-487-9610
www.mccann.com

Key Financial Facts

2003 U.S. advertising revenue: $425 million
1-yr. growth rate: 16 percent

Personnel Highlights

Not available.

Key Facts

- Owned by the Interpublic Group of Companies.
- Has offices in more than 130 countries.

Overview

McCann-Erickson was formed in 1930 when A. W. Erickson merged with H. K. McCann Co. Its more famous work includes "Miller Time" and "It's the Real Thing" (for Coke). Today, the company that has since been rechristened McCann Worldgroup continues to do some notable work. Recent work out of various McCann offices includes campaigns for Microsoft (featuring a man in an MSN Bumblebee costume), Hotwire.com, and MasterCard. Other accounts include Avis and Budget Rent-A-Car (both owned by Cendant), Exxon Mobil, Gillette, and Black & Decker. The San Francisco office picked up a big new account, Texas Instruments, early in 2004.

McCann recently lost its T.G.I. Friday's and U.S. Coke Classic accounts, but more than made up for that with wins including Capital One, Pfizer's Bextra, and Nikon.

Ogilvy & Mather Worldwide

Worldwide Plaza
309 W. 49th Street
New York, NY 10019
Phone: 212-237-4000
Fax: 212-237-5123
www.ogilvy.com

Key Financial Facts

2003 U.S. advertising revenue: $272 million
1-yr. growth rate: 7 percent

Personnel Highlights

Not available.

Key Facts

- Owned by the WPP Group.

- Clients include IBM, Cisco, Mattel, Nestle, American Express, Miller, Castrol, Coca-Cola, Ford, SAP, and Volvo.

Overview

Ogilvy & Mather was founded in 1948 by advertising legend David Ogilvy. Among the agency's famous concepts, icons, and phrases are Schweppervescence, the Shell Answer Man, and "Don't leave home without it." More recently it created the Miller Lite ads depicting two beautiful women wrestling over whether the beer is good because it tastes great or because it's less filling. (The ads created a controversy that resulted in them being shelved early.) Though this agency does some good creative work, it's better known for less glamorous aspects of its business, including media buying and planning and direct response.

The agency has been going through some tumult as a result of overbilling a client. It paid a fine in 2002, but its problems are not yet over: In 2004, several executives were indicted and a former executive entered a guilty plea due to the scandal.

Wins in 2003 included Cisco, American Chemistry Council, Brown & Williamson, U.S. work for Dupont, and Hellmann's and Wishbone for Unilever Bestfoods. Existing clients including American Express, DHL, and Coca-Cola (the Sprite Remix account) increased spending. The agency also successfully defended the Sprite account. The big loss was AT&T Wireless. In 2004 the agency will lose the White House account, worth $150 million annually, due to Ogilvy's PR and legal woes coming out of the overbilling controversy.

Publicis USA

4 Herald Square
950 6th Avenue
New York, NY 10001
Phone: 212-279-5550
Fax: 212-279-5560
www.publicis-usa.com

Key Financial Facts

2003 U.S. advertising revenue: $217 million
1-yr. growth rate: 42 percent

Personnel Highlights

Not available.

Key Facts

- Subsidiary of Publicis Worldwide, which is owned by the Publicis Groupe.

- Clients include Abbott Labs, BMW, Bombay Company, Denny's, Ernst & Young, GlaxoSmithKline, Heineken, Hewlett-Packard, Nestle, Pfizer, Procter & Gamble, Sara Lee, Siemens, T-Mobile, and Wells Fargo.

Overview

Publicis was founded in 1926, when 20-year-old Marcel Bleustein opened shop in the Montmartre district of Paris. Today, the agency has grown to become Publicis Groupe, a gigantic media holding company. Publicis USA is the U.S. advertising network of the Publicis Groupe.

The agency won three of eight pitches in 2003, including Thomson/RCA and TBS Superstation. In addition, existing clients T-Mobile Sidekick, P&G Pharmaceuticals' female sex-drive drug Intrinsa, Abbott Laboratories' Humira, Sara Lee deli brands, and UBS gave the agency additional business. The agency also took on P&G

and Cadbury's business when its parent Publicis closed D'Arcy Masius Benton & Bowles. Losses included L'Oreal's Plenitude, ATA, and OfficeMax (the latter two due to the closing of the Chicago office of Publicis USA in late 2002), and existing client Fuji Film cut spending by more than a third. The agency also failed in reviews for American Skiing, Cotton, E-Trade, and Pfizer's Bextra and Zoloft.

Publicis USA has offices in New York, Seattle, Dallas, and Indianapolis. The New York office recently brought on a top creative team from Saatchi & Saatchi London. Publicis USA clients include BMW, Cellular One, Nestle, PowerBar, Ernst & Young, Siemens, and Whirlpool.

Publicis & Hal Riney

2001 Embarcadero
San Francisco, CA 94133
Phone: 415-293-2001
Fax: 415-293-2619
www.hrp.com

Key Financial Facts

2003 U.S. advertising revenue: $55 million
1-yr. growth rate: -5 percent

Personnel Highlights

Number of employees (2002): 231
1-yr. growth rate: not available

Key Facts

- Subsidiary of Publicis Worldwide, which is owned by the Publicis Groupe.
- Lost its most important account, Saturn, in 2002, and laid off some 100 employees as a result.

Overview

Publicis & Hal Riney, which is run separately from Publicis USA, traces its roots back to 1977, when Hal Riney formed his own branch of Ogilvy & Mather. Riney's creative reputation was cemented in the 1990s by its laid-back, documentary-like Saturn campaign. The agency's recent creative has not included any campaigns nearly so memorable, but it continues to do good work for Sprint PCS, in ads featuring a man in a trenchcoat resolving problems caused by bad cell-phone reception.

Wins in 2003 included 24 Hour Fitness, Jamba Juice, the San Francisco Opera, and Shopping.com. The big loss was the $20 million Siebel account.

One major goal for the agency is to win another car account to make up for the loss of Saturn. In 2002 it tried and failed to win Hyundai; in 2003 it lost out on the BMW Western dealer review.

Saatchi & Saatchi

375 Hudson Street
New York, NY 10014
Phone: 212-463-2000
Fax: 212-463-9855
www.saatchi.com

Key Financial Facts

2003 U.S. advertising revenue: $221 million
1-yr. growth rate: 21 percent

Personnel Highlights

Number of employees: 7,000
1-yr. growth rate: 0 percent

Key Facts

- Owned by the Publicis Groupe.
- Every other year, gives out a $100,000 Innovation in Communication Award.

Overview

Saatchi & Saatchi is named after the two English brothers who founded the agency in 1971. The agency used aggressive business practices to become one of the biggest firms in the industry by the 1980s, but it ran into problems in the late 1980s (e.g., client losses and debt due to formerly separate agencies being joined under one roof), and by 1995 the Saatchis were no longer part of Saatchi & Saatchi.

In 2001 the 30-year-old Saatchi & Saatchi San Francisco office closed shop, a victim of the dot-com blues. Still, the Saatchi & Saatchi network comprises some 130 offices in about 80 countries.

Wins in 2003 included the International Olympic Committee, Wyeth/MedImmune's FluMist, as well as new work for Toyota, General Mills, and Procter & Gamble. The agency's big loss was the $200 million Johnson & Johnson account; other losses included UBS, T-Mobile, and Pernod Ricard brands.

Saatchi absorbed some of the accounts and operations of D'Arcy Masius Benton & Bowles (including work for Procter & Gamble and General Mills), which was shut down by parent Publicis in late 2002.

TBWA/Chiat/Day

5353 Grosvenor Boulevard
Los Angeles, CA 90066
Phone: 310-305-5000
Fax: 310-305-6000
www.tbwachiat.com

Key Financial Facts

2003 U.S. advertising revenue: $219 million
1-yr. growth rate: 8 percent

Personnel Highlights

Not available.

Key Facts

- Owned by the Omnicom Group.
- Received an overall grade of A- in the 2003 *Adweek* Agency Report Cards.

Overview

In 2003, the flagship office in Playa del Rey, CA, won accounts including Pennzoil and five other brands for Shell Lubricants and Masterfoods' Skittles brand; the San Francisco office had wins including Ask Jeeves, a project for Fox Sports, and the Women's Tennis Association; and the New York office, which is trying to move out from under the shadow of the Los Angeles office, made big steps in that direction via wins including the $150 million Nextel account and leadership on the McDonald's global account. That same year, the New York office resigned Kmart over a pay dispute, and the L.A. office lost SM Satellite Radio and Coinstar. Existing clients Nissan and Sony PlayStation both increased spending in 2003, as well.

Recent notable creative includes the Apple iPod campaign featuring real iPod owners dancing to music they've stored on their iPods and ads for the Nextel "Done" campaign illustrating how walkie-talkies make communications more efficient. The agency also continues to do good work for Absolut, which has been a client for 22 years.

Wieden + Kennedy

224 NW 13th Avenue
Portland, OR 97209
Phone: 503-937-7000
Fax: 503-937-8000
www.wk.com

Key Financial Facts

2003 U.S. advertising revenue: $44 million
1-yr. growth rate: 5 percent

Personnel Highlights

Not available.

Key Facts

- One of the few important agencies that still isn't owned by a global media conglomerate.
- Portland office took home five Pencils from the 2003 One Show, for creative for Nike and Miller High Life.
- New York office took home three Pencils from the 2003 One Show, for creative for ESPN.

Overview

Weiden + Kennedy has been one of the hottest shops over the past decade or so. The agency made a name for itself with its work for Nike. At a time when other athletic shoe makers were running ads focused on the specific features of their shoes, Weiden + Kennedy's Nike ads broke ranks and focused on branding—giving consumers a sense of having an emotional attachment to the product.

The agency still makes its living by coming up with campaigns that are considered edgy and creative. Notable work in recent times includes a Nike ad featuring commentators giving a play-by-play as a streaker dodges his way across a soccer field, ESPN ads featuring office coworkers playing "shelfball," and Nike ads featuring LeBron James.

The agency had no losses in 2003, though it did resign the Amazon.com account after the client cut spending. Wins included image work for America Online, Belvedere and Chopin vodkas, and Time-Warner Mystro TV.

The agency now makes nearly half its money via its international offices, in London, Amsterdam, and Tokyo.

Y&R Advertising

285 Madison Avenue

New York, NY 10017

Phone: 212-210-3000

Fax: 212-490-9073

www.yr.com

Key Financial Facts

2003 U.S. advertising revenue: $338 million

1-yr. growth rate: 4 percent

Personnel Highlights

Not available.

Key Facts

- Owned by the WPP Group.

- Clients include Accenture, AT&T, ChevronTexaco, Citibank, Colgate-Palmolive, Ford, Kraft, Miller, NFL, Sony, Virgin, Wyeth, and Xerox.

Overview

Y&R Advertising is the U.S. arm of global advertising behemoth Young & Rubicam (itself among the WPP Group's holdings). The agency opened shop in Philadelphia in 1923, and in 1932 started the first research department in the business. In the 1950s Y&R was instrumental in arranging for corporate sponsorship of daytime soap operas. It also created such memorable advertising as the "Be a Pepper" campaign for Dr. Pepper and the Metropolitan Life Insurance ads featuring Snoopy from the Peanuts cartoons ("Get Met. It Pays.").

More recently, in 2003 the agency landing the big Burger King account—but tension over whether to focus on brand or product in ads resulted in the departure of the client. Wins that year also included global ChevronTexaco and Orbitz; losses included Jim Beam, Dupont's Teflon, and NASCAR.

The Y&R network is huge, comprising some 540 offices in 80 countries.

Other Agencies

Other Advertising Agencies

Agency	Headquarters	Website
Ackerman McQueen	Oklahoma City	www.am.com
Bartle Bogle Hegarty	New York	www.bartleboglehegarty.com
Berlin Cameron/Red Cell	New York	www.bc-p.com
Bernstein-Rein Advertising	Kansas City, MO	www.bernstein-rein.com
Butler, Shine, Stern & Partners	Sausalito, CA	www.bsands.com
Campbell-Ewald	Warren, MI	www.campbell-ewald.com
Campbell Mithun	Minneapolis	www.campbellmithun.com
Carmichael Lynch	Minneapolis	www.carmichaellynch.com
Cliff Freeman & Partners	New York	www.clifffreeman.com
Cramer-Krasselt	Chicago	www.c-k.com
Crispin Porter & Bogusky	Miami	www.cpbmiami.com
Dailey & Associates	West Hollywood, CA	www.daileyads.com
Doner	Southfield, MI	Not available
Euro RSCG Worldwide	New York	www.eurorscg.com
Fogarty Klein Monroe	Houston	www.fkmagency.com
GlobalHue	Southfield, MI	www.globalhue.com
Gotham	New York	www.gothaminc.com
Hill, Holliday	Boston	www.hhcc.com
The Kaplan Thaler Group	New York	www.kaplanthaler.com
Kirshenbaum Bond & Partners	New York	www.kb.com
MARC USA	Pittsburgh	www.marcusa.com
MARS Advertising Group	Southfield, MI	www.marsusa.com
The Martin Agency	Richmond, VA	www.martinagency.com
McKinney & Silver	Raleigh, NC	www.mckinney-silver.com

Other Advertising Agencies (cont'd)

Agency	Headquarters	Website
Mullen	Wenham, MA	www.mullen.com
The Richards Group	Dallas	www.richards.com
Rubin Postaer & Associates	Santa Monica, CA	www.rpa.com
Team One Advertising	El Segundo, CA	www.teamoneadv.com
TM Advertising	Irving, TX	www.temmc.com
WestWayne	Atlanta	www.westwayne.com
Zimmerman & Partners	Ft. Lauderdale, FL	www.zadv.com

These agencies focus on producing online advertising and marketing campaigns.

📂 Interactive Agencies

Agency	Headquarters	Website
Agency.com	New York	www.agency.com
aQuantive	Seattle	www.aquantive.com
Carat Interactive	Boston	www.caratinteractive.com
Critical Mass	Chicago	www.criticalmass.com
Connect@JWT	New York	www.digital.jwt.com
Digitas	Boston	www.digitas.com
DraftDigital	New York	www.draftdigital.com
Euro RSCG 4D	New York	www.eurorscg4d.com
FCBi	New York	www.fcb.com
Grey Interactive Worldwide	New York	www.greyinteractive.com
iDeutsch	New York	www.ideutsch.com
Modem Media	Norwalk, CT	www.modemmedia.com
OgilvyInteractive	New York	www.ogilvy.com/o_interactive
Organic	San Francisco	www.organic.com
R/GA	New York	www.rga.com
SBI.Razorfish	Salt Lake City	www.sbigroup.com/rzf.html
Tocquigny Advertising, Interactive + Marketing	Austin, TX	www.tocquigny.com
Tribal DDB	New York	www.tribalddb.com
Wunderman Interactive	New York	www.wunderman.com
Zentropy Partners	Los Angeles	www.zentropypartners.com

The Public Relations Agencies

- The Top Agencies

- Other Agencies

The Top Agencies

Following are profiles of ten top PR agencies in the United States.

Burson-Marsteller

230 Park Avenue South
New York, NY 10003
Phone: 212-614-4000
Fax: 212-598-6914
www.bm.com

Key Financial Facts

2002 revenue: $175 million (est.)
1-yr. growth rate: –32.5 percent (est.)

Personnel Highlights

Number of employees: 1,600
1-yr. growth rate: –20 percent

Key Facts

- Part of the WPP Group.

- In 2004, received an Honorable Mention in *PR Week*'s Multicultural Marketing Campaign award category for its work educating Hispanics on migraine headaches and promoting AstraZeneca's Zomig migraine treatment.

- Received an Honorable Mention in the Arts, Entertainment, and Media Campaign category from *PR Week* in 2004, for its work promoting the Latin Grammy Awards.

- Won the 2004 Global Campaign of the Year award from *PR Week* for its "The New Color of Money" campaign promoting new U.S. paper currency.

Overview

Founded in 1953, Burson-Marsteller made its reputation working for big Fortune 500 clients. However, an increasing reliance on New Economy clients spelled trouble for the firm when the dot-com market went bust. Several rounds of layoffs resulted from the downturn in business. Still, this is one of the biggest, strongest PR machines in the business.

Burson-Marsteller's expertise in negotiating crises for clients came to the fore in the aftermath of September 11, 2001; in response, the agency handled related PR for clients like American Airlines and Morgan Stanley. It dealt with crisis again for the U.S. Postal Service, when it had to deal with the post-9/11 anthrax scare. Corporate relations, health care, consumer relations, employee communications, change management, and corporate responsibility are among the firm's other areas of expertise. The firm is also known for its expertise in public policy work. Technology and Hispanic marketing are among the areas of business on the rise at Burson-Marsteller.

Burson-Marsteller is known for having strong professional development programs. In the past the firm has been known for being very hierarchical, but that has apparently changed in recent years.

Burson-Marsteller has a strong network of international offices. In the United States, the firm is the strongest in the New York market and is also strong in Chicago and Washington, D.C. The agency is part of Young & Rubicam, which is a member of the WPP Group.

Edelman

200 E. Randolph Drive

63rd Floor

Chicago, IL 60601

Phone: 312-240-3000

Fax: 312-240-2900

www.edelman.com

Key Financial Facts

2002 revenue: $152 million

1-yr. growth rate: not available

Personnel Highlights

Number of employees: 1,900

1-yr. growth rate: not available

Key Facts

- Received an Honorable Mention in 2004 in *PR Week*'s Healthcare Campaign of the Year award category, for its work in support of Abbott Laboratories' launch of its Humira rheumatoid arthritis drug.

- Received an Honorable Mention in 2004 in *PR Week*'s Investor/Financial Relations Campaign of the Year category for its work promoting Adidas-Salomon AG in the U.S. business and financial media.

- Won *PR Week*'s 2004 Best Use of the Internet award for its work in support of LowerManhattan.info, a website set up by the City of New York to collect and disseminate information to workers and residents in Lower Manhattan in the wake of the 9/11 terrorist attacks.

- Won *PR Week*'s 2004 Best Use of Broadcast award for putting together a cross-country trip by a man riding an MTD Yard-Man tractor mower, resulting in 52 million media impressions.

Overview

Edelman, which was founded in 1952 and today has some 1,900 employees, is the largest independent PR agency in the world—and one of the most well rounded, in terms of having a significant presence in a wide variety of markets and offering services such as research and advertising that others in the industry may not be able to offer.

Edelman reacted to the business downturn in the early 2000s by closing offices in some smaller markets, such as Milwaukee, Austin, and Houston and by laying off employees. However, the agency remains strong in the New York, Chicago, and Washington, D.C., markets.

The agency's expertise is strongest in consumer marketing and health care. It also has notable strengths in crisis management and public affairs.

Edelman has a reputation for being culturally entrepreneurial—more of a meritocracy and less bureaucratic than other big agencies—but in recent years it has been trying to develop more defined business processes and to develop more teamwork and collaboration among employees.

Fleishman-Hillard Inc.

200 N. Broadway
St. Louis, MO 63102
Phone: 314-982-1700
Fax: 314-231-2313
www.fleishman.com

Key Financial Facts

Not available.

Personnel Highlights

Number of employees: 2,300
1-yr. growth rate: not available

Key Facts

- Took home an Honorable Mention in 2004 in *PR Week*'s Product Brand Development Campaign of the Year award category, for its work promoting the 150th anniversary of piano maker Steinway & Sons.

- Received an Honorable Mention in 2004 in *PR Week*'s Corporate Branding Campaign of the Year category for its work on behalf of SBC, as well as the Corporate Branding Campaign of the Year award for its work on behalf of Graybar, a distributor of electrical, telecom, and networking products.

- Received an Honorable Mention in 2004 from *PR Week* in the Best Use of the Internet award category, for its work driving parents to the TheAntiDrug.com website, a site of the White House Office of National Drug Control Policy.

- Owned by the Omnicom Group.

Overview

Founded in 1946, Fleishman-Hillard has operations around the world, but it's best known for its strength in a variety of markets across the United States. In addition to St. Louis, the firm is strong in Chicago, New York, and Texas, among other markets. The agency has some 2,300 employees, more than 400 of them in the St. Louis office.

Areas of expertise include public affairs, health care, corporate communications, consumer marketing, and technology. Growth areas include health care, internal communications, and public affairs.

The firm is big on fostering a strong, collegial culture and has a reputation for producing high-quality work.

Hill and Knowlton, Inc.

466 Lexington Avenue
Third Floor
New York, NY 10017
Phone: 212-885-0300
Fax: 212-885-0570
www.hillandknowlton.com

Key Financial Facts

2003 revenue: $191 million
1-yr. growth rate: not available

Personnel Highlights

Number of employees: 1,096
1-yr. growth rate: not available

Key Facts

- Owned by the WPP Group.

- Won the 2004 *PR Week* Employee Communications Campaign of the Year award, for its work on behalf of International Truck and Engine Corp. during a period when union workers were threatening a strike; a new contract agreement was reached without a strike.

- Received an Honorable Mention in the 2004 *PR Week* Public Sector Campaign of the Year award category for its work educating voters in Pinellas County, FL, on how to use that county's new touch-screen voting system.

Overview

Founded in 1927, Hill and Knowlton is today part of the WPP Group. The firm is particularly strong in New York, Los Angeles, Washington, D.C., and Chicago.

The firm's biggest strength is its expertise in corporate communications, including crisis management, litigation, and employee communications. It's also strong in public affairs, especially in Chicago and Washington, as well as social marketing, especially in Los Angeles. It has a strong presence in vertical markets including technology, health care, financial services, and energy and utilities.

The culture of Hill and Knowlton is known for its emphasis on collaboration. Through the agency's Virtual Academy, employees can access excellent online training.

Ketchum

1285 Sixth Avenue
New York, NY 10019
Phone: 646-935-3900
Fax: 646-935-4499
www.ketchum.com

Key Financial Facts

Not available.

Personnel Highlights

Number of employees: 1,100+
1-yr. growth rate: not available

Key Facts

- Owned by the Omnicom Group.

- Received the 2004 Community Relations Campaign of the Year award from *PR Week* for its work on behalf of Project Homefront, a Home Depot program that provided home repair and maintenance assistance to the families of Home Depot employees serving in the military in Iraq.

- Received the 2004 Nonprofit Campaign of the Year award from *PR Week* for its work in support of the Carnegie Museum of Natural History's "DynoMite Day" event.

- Won *PR Week*'s 2004 Promotional Event of the Year award for its work on the 2003 Fiesta Bowl Tostitos Gold Halftime Challenge event, in support of the Tostitos Gold product launch.

- Winner of two Gold and one Silver SABRE awards in 2004.

Overview

Founded in 1923, Ketchum is an industry leader today. It was named the 2002 PR Agency of the Year by *PR Week*, which cited Ketchum's innovative use of technology, as well as its formal client-relationship methodology, saying, "This Agency of the Year award recognizes the fact that Ketchum has professionalized the practice of PR with clever planning tools and an intranet that has helped the agency conduct some impressive global campaigns."

The agency is particularly strong in the California (where it has offices in Los Angeles and San Francisco), New York, and Pittsburgh markets and is known for excellence in corporate reputation, consumer marketing, internal communications, and health care. Ketchum also has U.S. offices in Atlanta, Chicago, Dallas, and Washington, D.C., as well as an office in Toronto.

PR Agencies

Manning, Selvage & Lee

1675 Broadway
Ninth Floor
New York, NY 10019
Phone: 212-468-4200
Fax: 212-468-4175
www.mslpr.com

Key Financial Facts

2002 revenue: $95.4 million
1-yr. growth rate: −17.8 percent

Personnel Highlights

Number of employees (2002): 950
1-yr. growth rate: 2.7 percent

Key Facts

- Part of the Publicis Groupe.
- Named 2003 Agency of the Year by the Holmes Report.
- Received an Honorable Mention in the Consumer Launch Campaign of the Year category from *PR Week* in 2004, for its work promoting the switch from prescription to over-the-counter sales of Procter & Gamble's Prilosec heartburn medication.

Overview

Manning, Selvage & Lee has a strong presence in New York, Los Angeles, Chicago, Boston, Atlanta, and Detroit. Its areas of strength include health care, consumer marketing, technology, and corporate communications such as issues and crisis management, employee communications, and corporate reputation.

Manning, Selvage & Lee was founded in 1938. Today the firm is known for being collegial and respectful, but it also has a reputation for demanding a lot of work from employees.

In 2003 Manning Selvage & Lee was selected the agency of record for corporate reputation for Home Depot; this was among its most important business wins of the year.

Ogilvy Public Relations Worldwide

909 Third Avenue
New York, NY 10022
Phone: 212-880-5200
Fax: 212-697-8250
www.ogilvypr.com

Key Financial Facts

2002 revenue: $95 million
1-yr. growth rate: not available

Personnel Highlights

Number of employees: 978
1-yr. growth rate: not available

Key Facts

- Owned by the WPP Group.
- Won the Public Sector Campaign of the Year award from *PR Week* in 2004 for its "The Heart Truth" campaign for the National Heart, Lung, and Blood Institute.

Overview

Founded in 1980 as a subsidiary of the Ogilvy & Mather advertising agency, Ogilvy Public Relations today has nearly a thousand employees. It is the third-largest PR firm in the WPP family, after Burson-Marsteller and Hill and Knowlton.

The agency was particularly hard hit by the tech bust, and it had to close offices in Dallas, Boston, and San Diego. But Ogilvy PR is still strong in New York and Washington, D.C., in particular, as well as in Chicago, Denver, and San Francisco.

Ogilvy PR is known for excellence in health care, social marketing, technology, and corporate communications.

The agency is investing heavily in professional development for its employees.

Porter Novelli

450 Lexington Avenue
New York, NY 10017
Phone: 212-601-8000
Fax: 212-601-8101
www.porternovelli.com

Key Financial Facts

2003 revenue: $117 million
1-yr. growth rate: not available

Personnel Highlights

Number of employees: 1,004
1-yr. growth rate: not available

Key Facts

- Owned by the Omnicom Group.
- Clients include the American Cancer Society, PricewaterhouseCoopers, Gillette, GlaxoSmithKline, Pfizer, and Procter & Gamble.

Overview

Porter Novelli was founded in 1972 and today has some 1,000 employees. The firm made a lot of money from technology clients during the tech boom and so was hit hard by the decline in that sector.

The firm's biggest offices are its New York and Washington, D.C. locations. It is looking to San Francisco, Boston, and Atlanta for growth. Other U.S. office locations include Austin, Chicago, Fort Lauderdale, Irvine, Portland, Sacramento, San Diego, and Seattle. Around the world, Porter Novelli has offices in 89 cities in 50 countries.

Porter Novelli is strong in health care, consumer marketing, and technology. The firm is trying to grow its presence in corporate and public affairs.

Waggener Edstrom Inc.

3 Centerpointe
Suite 300
Lake Oswego, OR 97035
Phone: 503-443-7000
Fax: 503-443-7001
www.wagged.com

Key Financial Facts

2002 revenue: $59 million
1-yr. growth rate: not available

Personnel Highlights

Number of employees: 500
1-yr. growth rate: not available

Key Facts

- Winner of the 2004 PR Agency of the Year award from *PR Week*.
- Received an Honorable Mention in 2004 in *PR Week*'s Campaign of the Year award category for its work in support of AVI BioPharma's antisense therapeutic platform.

Overview

Waggener Edstrom is known as a leader in technology PR. The fact that Microsoft is a big client doesn't hurt, of course. In addition, it was one of the first PR firms to specialize in serving biotech concerns. It has been expanding in recent years—both by taking on more nontech work and by opening an office in the New York metropolitan region.

The firm has a reputation for treating its employees really well; employees enjoy profit sharing, tuition reimbursement, and excellent internal training. And the rank and file seem to be more in synch with management than is the case at many big agencies.

Weber Shandwick Worldwide

640 Fifth Avenue
New York, NY 10019
Phone: 212-445-8000
Fax: 212-445-8001
www.webershandwick.com

Key Financial Facts

2002 revenue: $339.8 million

1-yr. growth rate: −11.9 percent

Personnel Highlights

Number of employees: 3,000

1-yr. growth rate: not available

Key Facts

- Part of the Interpublic Group of Companies.

- Winner of the 2004 *PR Week* Campaign of the Year award for its work promoting the law firm Foley & Lardner as a provider of solutions to help corporations deal with new corporate-governance and accounting rules arising out of the Sarbanes-Oxley Act of 2002.

- Took home an Honorable Mention in 2004 in *PR Week*'s Public Affairs Campaign of the Year award category for its work for the Prairie Island Indian community, which resulted in a greater voice for island residents in discussions with Xcel Energy over toxic waste dumping on the island and incentives for Xcel to begin removing already-dumped waste.

- Received a 2004 Honorable Mention in *PR Week*'s Crisis/Issues Management Campaign of the Year award category for its work helping Case Western Reserve University after an armed man took 100 people hostage on campus.

Overview

Weber Shandwick, which is part of the Interpublic Group, is the world's largest PR agency. It was formed in 2001, when Interpublic combined PR players Weber Shandwick Worldwide and BSMG Worldwide after acquiring BSMG's parent company, True North. Initially there was worry that the merger would be troublesome, but in the end the two firms came together smoothly.

Weber Shandwick's areas of expertise include consumer marketing, health care, corporate communications, entertainment marketing, and technology.

The firm is a major force in almost every first- and second-tier market in the country; the exceptions are southern markets such as Atlanta and Miami. Internationally, the agency has a strong presence in locations such as Belgium, Germany, Italy, Japan, Hong Kong, Singapore, Spain, and the United Kingdom.

The firm is known for its commitment to the communities in which it does business. For two decades, the Minneapolis office has been putting 5 percent of pretax earnings back into the community through a pro bono program. More recently, offices such as Washington, D.C., New York, and Hong Kong have started their own giving-back programs.

One big change in the way Weber Shandwick does business has been its recent shift from managing accounts by practice area and geographic location to centralizing management of big clients.

Other Agencies

Other PR Agencies

Agency	Headquarters	Website
Capstrat	Raleigh, NC	www.capstrat.com
Carmichael Lynch Spong	Denver	www.carmichaellynchspong.com
Chandler Chicco Agency	New York	www.ccapr.com
CKPR	Orlando	www.ckpramplified.com
Cone	Boston	www.coneinc.com
Creative Response Concepts	Alexandria, VA	www.crc4pr.com
DeVries Public Relations	New York	www.devries-pr.com
Dittus Communications	Washington, D.C.	www.dittus.com
Dix & Eaton	Cleveland	www.dix-eaton.com
Dorland Global Health Communications	Philadelphia	www.dorland.com
Edward Howard & Co.	Cleveland	www.edwardhoward.com
Euro RSCG Life NRP	New York	www.erlnrp.com
Euro RSCG Magnet	New York	www.eurorscg-magnet.com
French I West I Vaughan	Raleigh, NC	www.fwv-us.com
Gibbs & Soell Public Relations	New York	www.gibbs-soell.com
Golin/Harris	Chicago	www.golinharris.com
G.S Schwartz & Co.	New York	www.schwartz.com
The Hoffman Agency	San Jose, CA	www.hoffman.com
Horn Group	San Francisco	www.horngroup.com
Jasculca/Terman and Associates	Chicago	www.jtpr.com
M Booth & Associates	New York	www.mbooth.com
Makovsky & Company	New York	www.makovsky.com
Marina Maher Communications	New York	www.mahercomm.com

Other PR Agencies (cont'd)

Agency	Headquarters	Website
Morgan & Myers	Jefferson, WI	www.morganmyers.com
MWW Group	East Rutherford, NJ	www.mww.com
Padilla Speer Beardsley	Minneapolis	www.psbpr.com
Paine PR	Los Angeles	www.painepr.com
PAN Communications	Andover, MA	www.pancommunications.com
Peppercom	New York	www.peppercom.com
Publicis Dialog	New York	www.publicisdialog.com
Rogers & Associates	Los Angeles	www.rogersassoc.com
Rowland Communications Worldwide	New York	www.rowland.com
Sloane & Company	New York	www.sloanepr.com
Spectrum Science Public Relations	Washington, D.C.	www.spectrumscience.com
Stanton Communications	Washington, D.C.	www.stantoncomm.com
Stanton Crenshaw Communications	New York	www.stantoncrenshaw.com
Text 100 Public Relations	San Francisco	www.text100.com
Vollmer Public Relations	Houston	www.vollmerpr.com
Widmeyer Communications	Washington, D.C.	www.widmeyer.com

On the Job

- Inside an Advertising Agency

- The Making of an Ad

- Inside a Public Relations Agency

- The Making of a PR Campaign

- Real People Profiles

On the Job

Inside an Advertising Agency

Following are descriptions of the key jobs in advertising, the career track for those who take them, and the skills you need to do the job well.

Account Management

The account management (also known as *account services*) department is the ad agency's primary contact with the client. It acts as a middleman of sorts, communicating the client's concerns to the various agency departments and the agency's thoughts and concerns to the client. In addition, the account team manages the execution of ads by coordinating the agency's resources to get ads made "on time, on budget, on strategy, and in a way that meets the client's needs," as an insider puts it. This might involve making sure the agency has received legal clearance to use the images and music in an ad or ensuring that ads in production are moving from department to department and then out the door.

While account management is a primarily administrative function at some agencies, most have a number of higher-level jobs in the department. For instance, the account team may be intimately involved in developing strategy for the client by using its understanding of the client's business, the consumer marketplace, and the agency's various capabilities to advise the client on strategy issues. Specifically, the account team might work with the account planning department and the creative department to develop a communication or creative strategy for what the client wants the marketplace to think and feel about it or its products, and with the media department to develop a media strategy for where the ads will be placed. The account team might assist the creative department in developing the concept for an ad or a campaign and also be responsible for selling the client on the creative department's work. (One insider says, "If you hate sales, don't go into account management.") The client reviews the agency's ideas, and the account team should have a deep understanding of the ads the creative department is proposing, so it can explain how the ads address the client's strategy.

With the rise of account planning in American advertising, some agencies' account management departments are ceding control of account strategy to account planning. An insider says, "Strategic planners [account planners] have taken on a lot of the strategic development that account management people used to do." Job seekers looking for account management jobs would be wise to find out the departments' level of involvement at the companies they are interested in.

Career Path

At some agencies, being an administrative assistant is the only entry-level path into account management. At others, account coordinator is the entry-level position. Still other agencies start new employees in the assistant account executive position. After that, the career path looks like this:

- Account executive
- Account manager
- Account supervisor
- Management supervisor
- Vice president
- Director

At the entry level, most positions in account management will be, at least in part, glorified secretarial jobs in which you make sure ads move smoothly through the execution process. Depending on the agency and the manager, you may have some competitive-analysis responsibility or be invited along to client

On the Job

meetings or ad shoots. But as an insider says, "The lower you are on the account totem pole, the more it's about execution. The higher you are, the more it's about strategy."

Skill Set

People entering account management must have strong social skills, since a good chunk of their job involves managing people. As one insider says, "As you move up in account management, one of your responsibilities becomes managing the people below you. But even at the lower levels, you're managing people in other departments." People with their sights set on account management should also be organized and good at multitasking, because they'll be working on a variety of things simultaneously. In addition, account management candidates should have a good understanding of marketing and selling, since the job is about helping clients sell their goods and selling the agency to the clients. They should also be able to think like both business people and creatives, since they have to deal with both camps. According to an insider, "In terms of personality, creatives and clients are often diametrically opposed. . . . And the better direction you give the creatives, the better ads you get." Finally, it helps to have an eye for talent to make sure the agency's best creative work makes it into the final ads.

A final note regarding the account management skill set: Agencies are looking for account people who don't have ambitions to be art directors or copywriters. "Don't go into account management if you really want to be a creative," an insider says—you'll only end up being frustrated by your job.

Account Planning

The job of an account planner is to gain a deep understanding of the consumer in order to improve the service the agency offers its clients. Just as the account management department's job is to know the client, the account planning department's job is to know the consumer.

In many agencies, account planning has taken the place of the old research department, which gathered statistical information about consumers' likes and dislikes. Account planning is different from research in two main ways: For one thing, account planners are intimately involved in devising strategy for the client, in a way researchers never were. And account planners aim for a deeper understanding of the consumer than researchers did. While the researcher could talk about the whats and hows of consumer behavior, the account planner's job is to get inside the consumer's head and understand the whys of consumer behavior. In other words, the account planner has to not only know that the urban male 18- to 25-year-old market likes to wear baggy pants that ride low on the waist, but also that the market prefers those pants because they are a renegade, gangsta rejection of baby boomer fashion.

Account planners conduct both quantitative and qualitative research. The quantitative research is what a straight-research department might do: compiling statistics about who behaves how and who buys what. The qualitative research is where the "why" comes in. This involves conducting focus groups with a client's target consumers to find out what they like and don't like about the products of the client and those of its competitors. Some account planners go even deeper into the research; one insider tells of how a representative of an agency with a video-game account would hang out with boys while they played video games to get a feel for what they liked about the games they played. The account planner might also conduct research as part of the agency's effort to develop the strategy for an account and to test how the target market will respond to ads before they run.

Career Path

The typical account planning career path is as follows:

- Junior account planner
- Senior account planner
- Vice president
- Director

As you progress, you generally move from doing grunt work to planning strategy. Expect to be low-paid early in your account planning career. If you do well, however, you can advance rapidly.

Skill Set

Good account planning people need an intuitive understanding of human psychology and a curiosity about what makes people tick. They need an understanding of marketing and an ability to clearly translate their thoughts into words, since they write the creative briefs that focus the goals of the agency's creatives. In addition, it's important to get along well with people, as they conduct focus groups and deal with the client and other departments in the agency. And the account planner must have strong analytical skills to glean meaning from mountains of data.

If this sounds like you, you might do well in account planning. But beware: It's extremely difficult to find an entry-level position in account planning. Although some agencies hire people just out of school for junior planning positions, the vast majority only hire candidates from account planning in other agencies or those who move laterally from within the agency.

Creative

In most agencies, the creative department's job is to turn the strategy for an account into concepts that can be made into finished ads. (In the more creative-driven agencies, the creative department may have a significant role in devising the client's strategy.) Usually, once the client's strategy has been decided on, the agency will assign one or more creative teams to develop concepts that support the strategy. For example, if a discount department store has a strategy of attracting a higher-end clientele, the creative team might come up with a concept showing well-dressed people driving up to the store in expensive cars and then emerging from the store with the surprisingly highbrow products the store now carries.

A creative team consists of a copywriter and an art director. In theory, the copywriter supplies the words and the art director supplies the images, but it never really works that way. Either member of a creative team can come up with the words or images. What's really important is that the creative team produces strong ideas that meet the client's strategy.

Since the creatives are considered the agency's most prized resource—after all, the strength of an agency's ads is driven by the strength of the ideas coming from its creative department—the people in these positions often seem pampered: Although everyone else is wearing suits or business-casual attire, the creatives often saunter in wearing jeans and Hawaiian shirts. While the assistant account executive is going over columns of numbers in a budget and the junior media buyer is on the phone negotiating rates with a newspaper's ad rep, the creatives might be sitting down the hall howling at jokes. Creatives often come in later than the people in account management and planning—and leave earlier. They might go to lunch for several hours in the middle of the day or head out to a sunny spot in a nearby park to jot down ideas. As one creative says, "When it's not busy, I don't really have to be at the office."

Unless, of course, there's a deadline. In that case, the jokes will be fewer, and the creatives might work all night honing concepts before a pitch for a new account. Creatives also have to deal with office politics, especially when several creative teams are pitted against each other to come up with concepts for the same account. And creatives are frequently frustrated by clients who don't have an eye for good creative work or who are too conservative or narrow-minded. Just about every creative in the business can tell you about how some of his or her best work was killed by the client.

All the frustrations can be worth it, though. While creatives start out at a low salary, they can advance in a hurry in both pay and title. All it takes is one breakout campaign or one big award to make a used Volvo–driving junior copywriter into a new sportscar–driving senior copywriter. And people in the creative department are on the front lines of popular culture, producing the images and language that shape the way people think and speak. Imagine composing a line that becomes part of the vernacular, such as, "I can't believe I ate the whole thing," or "Where's the beef?" If that appeals to you, then you understand a big part of what attracts people to careers in creative.

Career Path

Beginning creatives start out as junior copywriters and junior art directors. If they're good, they eventually become senior copywriters and art directors. The creative director oversees the creative department. The only way to get a job in creative is to put together a book of sample ads. Some people take assistant positions in agency creative departments. There, they get advice from the agency's creatives while they put together the book that, they hope, will land them a job as a junior creative.

Others go through academic programs that help them put together a professional-looking book. And some people just put together their books themselves and are talented or lucky enough to land a job.

Skill Set

Most creatives are, well, creative—they generate ideas, and lots of them. Good creatives have the ability to discard their lesser ideas and are confident enough to be self-critical when necessary. They're also able to deal with a lot of criticism from others. An account management supervisor might criticize an art director's work, and even if she doesn't agree with the criticism, she must not take the criticism personally. Or an art director might think the latest idea from the copywriter he's teamed with is worthless. If he can't tell the copywriter what he thinks, then the two are not going to work very well as a team.

Good creatives also must have good marketing sense and communication skills. After all, creatives have to sell the ads to both the agency's account management people and the client's marketing people, as well as work with the production department to get the finished ads as close to the original vision as possible.

Media

Media is in charge of putting the agency's ads where they will most effectively reach their targeted market. This was essentially the original business of advertising agencies: acting as a liaison between advertisers and the media. The ad agency would take the finished ad given to it by a client and place it in newspapers and magazines. Today, media is still a big part of advertising, but it's more intense and focused than ever. Some agencies do nothing but media planning and buying; many clients will split an account, giving the creative side to one agency and the media responsibilities to another.

The media department has two responsibilities: planning and buying. Media planners decide where to place ads—in which media, when, and for how long. Account management tells the media planner what audience the client wants to reach and what the budget is. The media planner then does research to learn about the target market's media habits. Do people in the target market typically watch TV during the day or at night? Do they watch sporting events, soaps, or game shows? Which newspapers or magazines do they read? Based on the answers to these questions and countless others like them, media planners decide where to place the ads. For example, if part of a client's strategy is to reach wealthy people in San Francisco, but the media budget is light, the media plan might call for outdoor advertising in a well-to-do neighborhood such as Pacific Heights.

When the media plan has been written and the advertisements executed, it's the media buyer who actually places the ads and negotiates the prices to run them. Media works primarily with account management, but they might also interact with production and creative to determine whether an ad can be executed in time to run in a particular spot.

Career Path

The career path in media looks something like this:

- Media assistant (a clerical position)
- Assistant media planner or buyer
- Media planner or buyer
- Senior media planner or buyer
- Media supervisor
- Vice president
- Director

Media is also a good foot-in-the-door path into the other business areas within advertising, such as account management and account planning. The pay can be horrendous at first, but a good chunk of the entry-level opportunities in advertising exist here.

Skill Set

People who do well in media have good analytical skills to help them analyze media research and determine where to best place ads. They are detail-oriented and comfortable with numbers and tend to have a good understanding of marketing.

Production

Production is the actual physical making of the ads. Depending on the size of the agency, some or all of this work may be contracted to outside firms. When an ad agency is making a TV ad, for instance, it's common to hire an outside director who works through an independent TV commercial production company. Most agencies produce print ads (and storyboards for TV ad pitches) in-house, though, and hire computer-savvy graphic artists to do the work. The production department generally has the most contact with the account management and creative departments. The higher you rank within the production department, the more say you'll have in design issues. The closer you are to entry level, the more your work will consist of grunt layout tasks.

The production department can also be a path into other areas of advertising. It's a good place for young graphic artists to learn about advertising and get to know people who can advise them on how to put together a book.

Traffic

Some larger agencies have so many people working on so many different ads that they need a separate department just to handle the movement of ads between departments. This is called the *traffic* department. Positions here don't require much in the way of education, creativity, or specialized skills. Mainly, you need to be organized, responsible, and detail-oriented. This is a good way to learn the ins and outs of how an agency works, and many people in traffic end up moving into other areas of advertising.

New Business

In many agencies, members of senior management are responsible for attracting new business; some larger agencies have distinct new business departments. The role of the new business department is to keep track of possible new clients and to marshal the agency's resources when putting together a pitch for a new client. The work can be intense and the hours long—after all, new business is the lifeblood of the advertising agency. The entry-level position is coordinator, a largely clerical job.

The Making of an Ad

Now that you understand how an advertising agency is structured, we can better explain just how the business works. To help with this, we've come up with an imaginary product scenario. It goes like this: It's sometime in the near future, and hand puppets have become a hot item in the marketplace. First teens started buying them and wearing them to school and to parties. But now, several years into the craze, the market for hand puppets, while still huge, has stopped growing. And Five Fingers Inc., one of the big manufacturers of hand puppets, has seen its sales decline slightly.

Winning New Business

Five Fingers is so dissatisfied with the market performance of its hand puppets that it has decided to introduce a new line of fleece hand puppets to see whether they will increase sales. Five Fingers has also decided that it needs to shake up its advertising to give itself a new image among hand puppet consumers. So it's put its account, which has been at the same agency for years, up for review.

This news ripples quickly through the advertising world. Five Fingers is renowned in the hand-puppet industry and was the first manufacturer to offer hand puppets with double-stitched seams. What a coup it would be for any advertising agency to win this account! Instantly, every agency in the industry sends Five Fingers a proposal indicating its interest in the account and the resources it can bring to the new Five Fingers campaign. From that list, Five Fingers chooses several agencies from which it wishes to hear new-campaign proposals.

On that shortlist is our agency: The Agency. The Agency is a full-service shop with clients in a variety of industries. It has shown that it can help clients increase sales through its understanding of the consumer marketplace, its ability to strengthen clients' branding, its cutting-edge creative work, and its ability to get ads in front of the people it wants to reach.

Teams of people from all departments at each of the short-listed agencies go feverishly to work coming up with proposals for strategy, concept, and execution for the Five Fingers account. One by one, the teams on the shortlist make their pitch to Five Fingers executives. In the end, Five Fingers decides that it likes The Agency's pitch best.

Servicing the Client

Now Five Fingers is The Agency's account, and it's time to go to work on strategy, concept, and execution. Some of this work has already been done as part of the pitch to Five Fingers. The Agency has already come up with a strategy; a concept for turning that strategy into ads, mock radio scripts, TV-ad storyboards, and print ads; and a preliminary plan for getting the ads in the right media. But now there's more time and, thanks to meetings with Five Fingers' marketing executives, a deeper understanding of the client. Not to mention, more money.

Strategy

Account management and account planning are the primary strategists at The Agency. Account management, working with the client's marketing team, decides that Five Fingers' planned strategy of pushing the fact that fleece hand puppets wick moisture away from the skin is not going to work. It's time for a new strategy—one that focuses on brand image and not product benefits. But what should that be, exactly?

Account management looks at the market research and realizes that while young adults are still buying Five Fingers hand puppets, today's teenagers are buying hand puppets made by smaller upstart manufacturers. It also learns that while young adults buy new hand puppets only when their old hand puppets wear out, teenagers are likely to own multiple hand puppets. Together with Five Fingers' marketing department and The Agency's creatives, account management devises a new strategy: to win a greater share of the teen hand-puppet market.

Next, account planning fine-tunes the strategy. It has learned from focus group research that today's teens want to buy hand puppets that are cool and don't want anything to do with hand puppets that they consider old-school. With account planning's help, the strategy becomes to position Five Fingers' new fleece hand puppets as outside the mainstream—a difficult task, considering that Five Fingers is one of the major players in the hand-puppet market. And the task is made even more difficult by the client's insistence that the ads emphasize the fact that the new hand puppets wick moisture away from the skin.

Working with media, account management devises a media strategy for Five Fingers' fleece hand-puppet campaign. No longer will Five Fingers run its ads during TV shows like *Will & Grace*—shows aimed primarily at the twenty- and thirty-something crowd. Instead, Five Fingers ads will be placed in edgier alternative media outlets—like the extreme sports magazine *Street Luge Monthly*, the teen fashion magazine *Whatever*, and TV shows like MTV's *The Real World–Fresno*.

Concept

Concept is where the creative department takes over the process. Account management and account planning give creative the creative brief, which states that the strategy on this account is to position Five Fingers' new line as the alternative to mainstream hand puppets. With that in mind, creative goes to work on the TV spot that will launch the campaign.

The creative team working on the account quickly comes up with what it thinks is a good concept: A girl rejects a couple of guys who are flirting with her in favor of a third guy who's wearing a Five Fingers fleece hand puppet.

Excited, the creative team develops the ad idea further. In the newer version, the girl is a high school sophomore and the two guys are seniors and stars on the football team. They drive up alongside the girl in a convertible, wearing "traditional" hand puppets (one wears a cotton hand puppet; the other's is made of wool). The guys start to flirt with the girl, but then their hand puppets start to bother them in the heat. Just as a look of disgust is starting to wash over the girl's face, a third guy rides up on a moped. He's wearing a Five Fingers fleece hand puppet, and his hand is nice and cool despite the heat. Even though he's a couple of years younger than the football players, the girl climbs on the moped seat, leaving the football stars sitting there, stunned.

The creative team really likes this idea. They know from their own understanding of our culture and from account planning that today's teens reject the traditional symbols of success like convertibles and football stardom. And the ad they've conceived has the added bonus of pointing out that Five Fingers fleece hand puppets will keep your hands cool in the heat. The only problem: The creative team can't come up with a good tag line. The best they've come up with so far is "Five Fingers. The Coolest." But it's too obvious, and they'd prefer something subtler, something that lets the ad just show how cool the new hand puppet is.

And then a new tag line hits them: "Not your older brother's hand puppet." Now the ad seems just about right. It says, "Five Fingers hand puppets are fresh and new," but doesn't hit you over the head like a sledgehammer.

The next step is to present the idea to the client. At the creative presentation, the account team walks the client through the strategy: to target the teen market by making fleece seem hipper than old-style hand puppets, while pointing out that fleece wicks moisture away from the skin. Then creative walks the client through storyboards for the proposed TV ad.

The Agency is lucky. The client really likes the ad. The only problem: The client insists that the moped be removed from the ad. It seems the daughter of the Five Fingers CEO lost the feeling in her toes in a tragic moped accident a few years earlier. So the creatives rewrite the ad and put the younger boy on a BMX bike instead of the moped.

Execution

From this point on, the process is pretty straightforward. The agency hires a director and a TV commercial production company to produce the TV ad. The production company casts the actors, directs and films the ad, and edits it into a finished product. The Five Fingers' marketing team and The Agency's account and creative teams remain part of the process to ensure that the ad comes out right.

Two weeks after the shoot, the client has approved the final cut of the ad, media has purchased time on *The Real World–Fresno* and other hip youth-oriented TV shows, and the ad is on the air. Now it's time to go to work on the Five Fingers print campaign.

Inside a Public Relations Agency

Day to day, PR pros "pitch" story ideas to reporters, trying to elicit coverage of subjects that are important to their clients. They also serve as company spokespeople, plan and hold events intended to generate publicity, and develop strategies that will spark media interest. An actress's appearance at an awards ceremony wearing nothing but a potholder, for instance, could be a PR ploy to get her in the papers.

Those with more experience in PR write speeches, prepare client executives for event appearances (making sure they understand the "messaging" they want to convey at the event), strategize the best time to announce a new product, work alongside an advertising agency to position products in the mind of the public, develop and publish newsletters, and manage crises, endeavoring to put a positive spin on events for a client organization. And along with representing the client to the public, PR practitioners represent the public to the client, helping the client understand the public's wants, needs, and concerns.

If you go into PR, you'll either work at an agency or within a larger company's communications department. At an agency, you'll serve multiple clients; at a large company, you'll serve that company—or, more likely, a division or area within it.

Within corporate PR departments, you'll probably work more independently than you will at an agency—which may lead to a sense of isolation but will give you plenty of opportunities to learn. Salaries are typically bigger in corporate PR. At an agency, you'll have exposure to a wider range of clients, which means the work is likely to be more interesting over time. Typically, you'll receive more mentoring as well.

On the Job

Career Path

Most people enter PR as an account coordinator or, when in a company's communications department, as a PR coordinator. Generally the account coordinator plays an administrative role, supporting an account executive. The work involves projects such as clipping newspapers, assisting in research, maintaining a list of media contacts, and coordinating mailings of press packets to the media. Generally, the account coordinator role is a stepping-stone to becoming an account executive.

The account executive works directly with the client, writing press releases, planning special events, preparing annual reports, and communicating regularly with the client. Often, the account executive tracks trends, looking for opportunities for the client to receive media coverage related to a widely covered news event, following up with the media once a press release has been sent, and organizing events. Account executives are sometimes called PR *specialists* in the communications department of larger organizations. In many instances, an account executive will represent a company at press conferences, write speeches or op-ed pieces for the company's CEO, prepare the annual shareholder report, and submit the client's products for industry awards.

A step up from the account executive is the account manager. The account manager oversees PR accounts, often managing the account executives and account coordinators. They'll often do hands-on executorial work similar to that handled by the account executive, but they'll oversee other staff members assigned to the account as well.

At the vice president and director level, you'll typically manage the firm, meet with higher-level clients, and create overall communication strategies. You'll be responsible for pitching accounts—that is, finding new clients—and making sure everything is working to the satisfaction of existing customers. You'll also be thinking up new communication services you can sell to existing clients. Within agencies, you'll work closely with younger staff to train and mentor them.

Many in PR are specialists in either a client industry or a specific PR function, if not both. For instance, Waggener Edstrom specializes in tech clients, meaning you'd better enjoy and show a passion for the technology industry if you want to work there. Other major industry specializations include health care, government, sports, entertainment, pharmaceuticals, and telecommunications.

In terms of specific PR functions, many PR professionals specialize in areas that include consumer marketing (launching clients' new products and supporting existing products), consumer affairs (which is concerned with issues of consumer safety and quality), investor relations (which involves the encouragement of investment in client organizations and generally requires an understanding of the financial markets), employee or labor relations (communication by clients' management to their workers), crisis management (the management of the client company's public image through a period that is fraught with the probability of getting bad press—think: Martha Stewart Omnimedia after her indictment for securities fraud), cause marketing (in which the client company associates its name—and probably its money—with a public cause like AIDS awareness or stopping underage drinking), litigation communications (managing communications when a client is suing someone or is being sued), government relations (lobbying on behalf of the client via government-agency contacts and the press), and media relations (which involves dealing with the press on a full-time basis).

Skill Set

Recent Graduates

To get in, you'll need a good general education and the proven ability to communicate well both in writing and speech. One insider says, "I can't think of a single job interview I've had that didn't include a writing test." An English degree will help; so will training in marketing, communications, and writing. Some universities offer public relations degrees.

You'll also need to have good people and social skills. Doing PR is all about relationships; to get newspaper and magazine reporters to take your calls, you've got to have a good relationship with them. And people skills also come in handy as far as working as a partner with the client. According to another insider, if you're shy, you may want to look elsewhere for a career. Public relations requires an outgoing personality, because it deals so much with reaching out to the press and to others to tell your client's story (or your company's story, if you're working in-house in a company's corporate communications department).

To excel, you'll also have to be entrepreneurial. Creative PR efforts seem to be heard over the general PR noise, and creative PR efforts require the risk-taking, hard work, and passion that entrepreneurs typically bring to the table.

Midcareer Candidates

If you want to break into PR midcareer, you'll the skills outline above. In addition, to make a lateral move, you'll probably have to bring along a deep inside knowledge of one or more industries. Knowledge of mass media and how they work is also relevant—many journalists make the switch to public relations. Folks like lawyers, management consultants, former government officials, and academics tend to do well when moving into PR.

Breaking In

The best way to get a foot in the door is to do an industry internship. Many PR agencies and big corporations' communication departments offer internship opportunities where you'll learn how to make contacts in the business and build up a portfolio. Experts say that PR is as much art as science, and the only way to get the skills is by practicing them. While you can break in from another field, unless you have media experience, you're probably going to have to start low on the ladder.

The Making of a PR Campaign

First World Financial, a stock brokerage catering to small investors, has just merged with The Capital Group, a financial manager for high-net-worth individuals, forming FirstWorld Capital. The new company hopes to make a mint in commissions on trades made by The Capital Group's client base, while turning existing First World Financial accounts into full-service financial-management clients. To help with determining its strategy and getting word of its new direction out to the public, FirstWorld Capital employs the services of an agency we'll call The PubliComm Group.

External Strategy

To position the newly merged company in the minds of existing clients, the media, the investment community, and the public at large—to make the world aware of its new capabilities and to differentiate it from straightforward brokerage firms and financial management companies —PubliComm creates a series of targeted messages. The core message is that there are powerful synergies at work in the combination of First World Financial and The Capital Group—that the new entity is greater than the sum of its parts. For small investors, the message is that FirstWorld will help them grow wealthier as they age—and is the perfect company for them to turn to for financial management expertise. For high-net-worth individuals, the message is designed to take advantage of the trend among individual investors to get more involved in managing their investments: that investors can now make trades with FirstWorld Capital, a company they should associate with smart investments.

On the Job

Campaign Execution

Next, PubliComm begins getting these messages out to the world. It writes press releases, prepares media kits, and talks to media contacts, announcing the expanded capabilities available to clients of FirstWorld Capital. It preps FirstWorld Capital executives on the messaging strategy. Soon, stories about FirstWorld Capital's new direction are appearing in newspapers and magazines from the *Atlanta Journal-Constitution* to *Money* magazine, and pieces targeted at high-net-worth individuals appear in the *Wall Street Journal* and the business section of the *New York Times*.

Internal Strategy

At the same time, FirstWorld Capital is struggling to integrate the cultures of its two legacy companies. First World Financial was known for its brash, entrepreneurial—some would say swashbuckling—style. The Capital Group was known for having a staid, careful culture. To help integrate the two cultures, FirstWorld enlists the aid of PubliComm's employee relations specialists. PubliComm conducts focus groups with employees of the two legacy companies and studies how other merged companies have handled issues of cultural integration. Then, with input from PubliComm, FirstWorld decides on its postmerger internal messaging. The core of the message is that in the new FirstWorld Capital, employees get the best of both worlds. The independent, entrepreneurial types from First World Financial will now be able to leverage the strong reputation of The Capital Group. And the former employees of The Capital Group will now be able to push the envelope in their jobs and will be rewarded for entrepreneurial efforts and energy.

Outcomes

The campaigns work wonderfully. At the end of the first year after the merger, business is up at FirstWorld Financial, among both small investors and high-net-worth individuals. Investors in the firm have taken the synergies message to heart, and the company's stock price is up as well. And the integration of the two component cultures of the firm has gone smoothly, with morale high among staff.

Real People Profiles

Advertising Account Manager

Years in business: 9

Education: BBA in marketing

Hours per week: 50

Size of company: 1,000 employees

Annual salary: $75,000

What do you do?

I'm the liaison between the agency and the client. I'm responsible for advertising strategy and advertising production.

How did you get your job?

I had an internship in college and used my contacts there to get an interview at another agency after graduation. I took a second internship at the second agency, which became an account coordinator job. I spent 5 years at that agency and then went to work for an old boss who'd moved to a third agency. Eventually I went to work for an industry acquaintance at my current agency. So it's been all about networking for me.

What are your career aspirations?

I want to manage strategy—to be the key consultant on products' marketing and advertising strategy. Long term, I can see myself either at an advertising agency or on the client side.

What kinds of people do well in this business?

People who can manage their egos and be team players. People with a good likeability quotient. People who are patient and passionate at the same time—a tough balance to find.

What do you really like about your job?

No two days are the same. I look forward to the uncertainty and to the challenges of managing the client's marketing. I also like the fact that we do killer creative. And I like that I can see the results of my work almost immediately.

What do you dislike?

Being treated like a vendor by the client. And when we get blamed for what are really other business issues—like when business is slow and the client assumes it must be the advertising's fault.

What is the biggest misconception about this job?

That it's Melrose Place. It's really fun, but there's also lots of hard work. If you're not dedicated and serious, it can chew you up. We lose 20 percent of our business every year. It's like constantly refilling a leaky bucket.

How can someone get a job like yours?

The key is an internship. For one thing, you'll make contacts that way. People who have been interns tend to get good jobs after graduation. And an internship can be a good test run in advertising. You'll get to know all about the business, about the different departments and what they do. That will benefit you, because your first couple of years in advertising will seem like boot camp—you don't want to go into advertising unless you know it's for the long term.

> " "
> **If you're not dedicated and serious, it can chew you up. We lose 20 percent of our business every year. It's like constantly refilling a leaky bucket.**

On the Job

A Day in the Life of an Advertising Account Manager

7:30   Check voice mail from home. Nothing. Head to work.

8:30   Arrive at the office; find two voice mails. One's from a soft drink client who's upset because he didn't see a TV spot we did on a program it was supposed to run on last night. The other is internal: An art director wants to use props that'll cost $4,000 more than is in the budget for a cola ad. Check my e-mail; I learn that my account coordinator is trying to find out if the mechanicals we sent to the client for approval yesterday have in fact been approved. This is reminder number 12 from the account coordinator.

8:45   Call media to have buyers check with TV stations and compare our buy with what actually happened with the soft drink ad last night.

9:15   Call art director to set up a meeting to decide whether the extra $4,000 in props is really necessary.

9:30   Call client's voice mail and leave a message saying we're checking on whether the spot ran last night and checking again on the mechanicals. E-mail account coordinator, telling her that I've left several voice mails with the client about the mechanicals during the past 20 hours.

10:00   Write creative brief for soft drink client's orange drink. The client wants to focus strategy on its new 11-ounce can, but focus groups show that people are much more interested in the fact that the drink contains 10 percent real fruit juice. My brief mentions the new can, but focuses on the real fruit juice angle.

12:30   Run downstairs for a sandwich, and eat it at my desk.

1:00   Get word from media that the cola spot ran as it was supposed to on TV last night. Call the client to pass on this information. Learn that the client didn't watch the last third of the program, when the spot aired.

1:30   Meet with art director. Decide that the $4,000 in props isn't really necessary to the cola ad, so I don't have to call the client to up the budget.

2:30   Client arrives at office for production meeting to review commercial directors' reels for an upcoming diet cola campaign, which will consist of six 30-second spots. I present the agency's recommendation of which director would be best. The client wants our second choice because he's $50,000 cheaper. Decide we need to do follow-up with production companies before making a decision.

4:00   Check e-mail. Media has sent me an e-mail about a print plan they just presented to the client. It seems the client would like to schedule rotations in their favorite magazine, *People*. Request a POV—point-of-view memo—from media discussing whether we should include *People* in this media plan. My gut feeling is that *People* is too expensive for this campaign. We're focusing more on regional coverage.

4:30   Call client. Leave message that we're looking into including *People* in the media plan.

5:15   Sit down with assistant account executive who's working on a competitive review—an advertising analysis of the soft drink market. Discuss ways to make the competitive review stronger.

6:00   Head home. Check voice mail from the car—nothing. I can eat dinner in peace tonight.

On the Job

Advertising Media Planner

Years in business: 3
Education: BA in English literature
Hours per week: 50
Size of company: 100 employees
Annual salary: $35,000

What do you do?

I create media plans. A client comes to me with a budget and a message it wants to get out. I find out who the target for that message is and figure out what the target group's media habits are. Then I decide what kind of media to use for the client's ads. I am also responsible for buying print ad space, so I negotiate rates for the print placements we buy.

How did you get your job?

Networking. My dad used to work for Dancer—an old ad agency—and he gave me the name of someone in the business when I moved here. I met with that person and quickly got a job as an assistant media planner. I was pretty clueless when I started; they had to explain to me what an advertising agency does.

What are your career aspirations?

I don't really know. I'm going to stick with this for a while. I think I might end up a teacher, but this is fun for now.

What kinds of people do well in this business?

You have to be organized in your thinking—analytical. You have to be able to look at data and draw conclusions from it. You also have to have a good eye for detail, because mistakes can cost the client real money. It also helps to be flexible; you will face roadblocks in the work and it helps not to feel gutted every time something goes wrong. It also helps to be good with numbers and people.

On the Job

What do you really like about your job?

I like the people I work with. My team is killer. But the best part is seeing the work get out there. It's pretty cool to see a campaign break on TV and in magazines. I also like the problem-solving aspects of the job.

What do you dislike?

Sometimes I dislike how convoluted the processes in an ad agency can be. Trying to get the ads through the agency efficiently can be really frustrating. I also get frustrated with numbers sometimes—for instance, when I can't get a budget to balance. And I don't like the pressure I sometimes feel not to make mistakes because I'm dealing with the client's money.

What is the biggest misconception about this job?

That it's only number crunching. People think it's like accounting. They think we just look in the book and pull out rates. That may have been how it was once upon a time, but now there are more aspects of the job that challenge you to think creatively.

How can someone get a job like yours?

Having connections to get in the door is really important. Once you land an interview, you need to show that you have common sense and that you'll be easy to work with.

A Day in the Life of an Advertising Media Planner

9:00   Arrive at work, check voice mail and e-mail. Call the agency's European offices to check on the media plans they owe us. (We give them the strategy on global campaigns, then they do the planning and buying and report back to us.)

10:00   Meet with a *BusinessWeek* rep to discuss an upcoming campaign and contracts.

10:30   Balance budgets on a search engine account. Responsibilities like this take a lot of my time.

11:00   Meet with account services and production to talk about upcoming deadlines. Try to make sure we can meet an insertion in an upcoming magazine issue. Give production the specs for the ad.

12:00   Lunch with a media rep from the *Wall Street Journal*. We take about 2 hours; it's a bit of business talk, but mostly just socializing. The rep is trying to build a relationship with me.

2:00   Status meeting with the entire media team. We update each other on the status of media planning and buying for different accounts.

2:30   Do runs on the computer to determine just who the target is on an account. I've gotten some guidance on this from the account services strategy brief, but I'm using syndicated research (information on different demographic groups) to get more focus on the target.

3:00   Start writing the media plan based on my research, the strategy brief, and the media budget for the campaign.

4:30   Go out riding the boards—checking out outdoor advertising locations—with the media buyer.

6:00   Head home.

Senior Advertising Copywriter

Years in business: 10

Education: BA in psychology and mathematics

Hours per week: 40

Size of company: 300 employees

Annual salary: $120,000

What do you do?

I create and oversee the production of print and broadcast advertising.

How did you get your job?

While I was working on Wall Street, I started taking portfolio classes at night. When I had a portfolio, I got my first job in the in-house advertising agency of a financial services company. From there I moved to writing direct mail at a better, more creative agency. Then I moved to a job writing ads at a less creative agency, and finally I ended up writing ads at my current agency—a full-service agency with a reputation for good creative.

What are your career aspirations?

I'm not anomalous in saying, "I've got to get the hell out of advertising." I'm interested in writing screenplays or fiction, directing a film, or maybe opening a bar. A lot of people have the aspiration to open their own ad agency; there are new creative boutiques popping up all the time. That idea has some appeal to me, too.

What kinds of people do well in this business?

Obviously, people who are very creative. It also helps to be energetic and theatrical. People who are witty, extroverted, and good at self-promotion seem to get ahead in advertising. This is not a good industry for the passive, unless they're very talented. You've got to be prepared to deal with constant criticism. You've also

> **You've got to be tuned into pop culture and understand a wide range of people, so you can write ads that appeal to different groups.**

got to be tuned into pop culture and understand a wide range of people, so you can write ads that appeal to different groups.

What do you really like about your job?

I have the ability to create things—to have a vision and then make it happen. Also, there's no set routine; I'm involved in all kinds of ads and all kinds of media. I do radio, TV, and print, and each entails different things, and I like that. I also really like working with music and film, and editing commercials.

What is the biggest misconception about this job?

A lot of people think advertising is a shameless, sell-anything business, and that there's this nefarious intent on the part of ad agencies to make people buy what they don't really want. That's so far from the kind of thinking that actually goes on in an ad agency. Mainly, we try to figure out what's good about products and then help the public see that.

How can someone get a job like yours?

Put a portfolio together. There are places you can go specifically for that purpose, that almost guarantee you a job when you finish. You'll leave those places with a polished portfolio, and these days that's what you need to get a job. When I look back now on my first portfolios, I find them laughable.

A Day in the Life of a Senior Advertising Copywriter

8:45   Get to work. Check e-mails and voice mails.

9:00   Conference call with account services and an automotive client regarding a spot that was just shot. The client has looked at the edit and doesn't like the way the characters are portrayed in it—says they're not friendly enough. The client also doesn't think the ad is funny enough.

10:00 Work with my partner, an art director, on new ideas for a soft drink account. Account services tells us the strategy is that this is a reenergizing drink. We start with some pretty literal representations of people being reenergized by the drink—for instance, a lecture hall full of snoozing students who are awakened every time the lecturer takes a sip of her soft drink. As we get into the process, we get a little less obvious and start having fun—conceiving of a soft drink SWAT team that charges in to help a couple of young guys with dangerously low energy who are not acknowledging good-looking women who walk by. This is a decent idea because the SWAT team is a concept that could translate across an entire campaign of ads.

12:30 Head around the corner for a burrito.

1:00 Drive to a recording studio to remix the voiceovers in a winery ad. As we wrote the ad, the characters were supposed to be kind of sarcastic, but the client wants us to mix in friendlier, more upbeat takes.

4:30 Handle a bit of paperwork for the upcoming 3-week credit card shoot in Australia and Thailand.

5:30 Head home.

Senior PR Account Executive

Years in business: 6

Education: BA in marketing communications

Hours per week: 45

Size of company: 30 employees in office (hundreds in agency in total)

Annual salary: $55,000

What do you do?

I do PR for an agency focused on technology clients. I keep up with the ins and outs of technology news; you've really got to know your industry. I write press releases. I spend hours on the phone talking to media contacts, trying to place stories about my clients and their products. I prep client executives before speaking engagements and sometimes sit in on meetings with media representatives in case the client runs into trouble.

How did you get your job?

I got my first job because of my college major. I went to job fairs, networked, responded to classified ads—the usual. Since then, it's been all about networking and industry contacts. I got my current job because I hated the last agency I worked for, and a friend at my current agency told me about a job opening here and then campaigned to get me hired.

What are your career aspirations?

For now, I enjoy PR. The people are great at this agency, and I like my clients. So I'd say I'd like to continue to advance in PR.

What kinds of people do well in this business?

First and foremost, you have to be a good communicator. You have to be able to write well, and every agency you approach for a job will make you prove your writing skill via a writing test before hiring you. Because you have to spend so much time talking to the press, you have to be a good speaker and be able to think on your feet.

What do you really like about your job?

At my current agency, I like the fact that management encourages us to have a good life-work balance. I've actually been scolded for staying too late at the office! But that's not the norm in the industry, and even here there are times when you have to work long, hard hours. I also like the fact that there are a lot of young people in my office and that we often go out together, to Happy Hours and things like that.

What do you dislike?

A really demanding client can make your life hell. And you can run into some a**holes in this business. My last boss had no social skills and would just start yelling at me for no reason. It got to the point that I started yelling back. I also dislike the way some members of the media treat you when you tell them you're in PR, either yelling at you or just hanging up on you. The fact is, they need us as much as we need them.

What is the biggest misconception about this job?

That if you're in PR, you're automatically part of some disinformation campaign. That can be true at times in some areas of PR, but where I am, I'm merely relaying information about my client's products to the marketplace, not spinning half-truths or lies. I'm proud of what I do.

How can someone get a job like yours?

A major in communications or marketing is really helpful in getting your first job. Doing an internship is also a great way to get your foot in the door. After that, it's all about networking.

A Day in the Life of a Senior PR Account Executive

8:30 Arrive at the office. There's a voice mail from my boss, who wants some changes made to a draft of a press release I wrote a couple of days ago. I go to work making the changes to the press release.

9:30 Show my boss the revised press release; she approves it.

10:00 Start calling technology writers to try to place stories about my client's new wireless device.

12:30 Lunch with some coworkers. We get sandwiches from a nearby deli and sit at an outside plaza to eat.

1:30 Receive a phone call from the client, who's still not happy with the press release I rewrote this morning. Buckle down to make still more changes.

3:00 More phone calls to the press.

5:00 I've made all the phone calls I can make today, so I take a little time to scan a few tech industry websites and magazines.

6:00 Time to head home.

The Workplace

- Lifestyle and Hours

- Culture

- Travel

- Compensation and Vacation

- Training

- Career Notes

- Insider Scoop

Lifestyle and Hours

People think of advertising as glamorous—and it can be. There are extravagant Christmas parties at the big agencies—one insider tells of being delighted when he got to his Christmas party and learned that Los Lobos would be the band. There are ballgames with the client, client dinners at excellent restaurants, 2-hour lunches courtesy of the magazine rep, trips to film on location in Fiji or Rio de Janeiro, and opportunities to befriend the famous people who star in the ads. (Look for a bit less extravagance than usual these days, though, as advertising agencies make like companies in every industry and look to cut costs.) There's also the constant opportunity to create an ad that makes a permanent mark on popular culture.

But that's not all there is to advertising. Behind the bright lights and the glitz are thousands and thousands of hours of hard work.

Those in PR, unfortunately, get all the hard work but usually significantly less glitz—though they can still get some fun perks, especially at big agencies with wealthy or plugged-into-the-scene clients, as well as the opportunity to create a buzz or contribute to a story that becomes part of popular culture.

While most people in advertising and PR work the kind of hours that get you home in time for dinner, when a deadline is approaching the hours can skyrocket. We're talking 90 hours a week during crunch times, conceivably. And when the client makes a request for an emergency press release or a revision to an ad? Well, you can kiss your dinner-and-a-movie date good-bye—and your weekend trip to the beach, too. Even advertising creatives, who can really slack off when they're not under gun, can be at the office until late at night when there's a deadline approaching. "I work between 35 and 90 hours a week," one creative says. "It's all project-based work, so it's feast or famine in terms of the hours."

Along with the hard work comes occasional high stress. You might be in advertising account management and freaking out because a mechanical that had to go out at 5:00 isn't ready yet at 5:15. You might be in advertising production and freaking out because the account executive who's waiting for you to finish that mechanical is standing over your shoulder, freaking out herself. You might be in PR and freaking out because the client-company executive you're supposed to brief before tomorrow morning's press conference is stuck in a meeting that's supposed to last well into the evening. And there's a lot of money riding on your work in an advertising or PR agency, so you don't want to make mistakes. "You have to be able to handle pressure," says insider. If you screw up—or even if you haven't, but some bigwig at your agency or the client thinks you have—you can end up out of a job in a hurry. And if your agency loses a key account, you might be handed a pink slip no matter how well you do your job.

Culture

So why do people go into advertising and PR? Again and again, insiders tell us the same thing: These industries can be a lot of fun. The people who are drawn to advertising and PR are either creative themselves or have a great appreciation for creative work. They're smart, curious, and into popular culture. They're also young. One advertising insider estimates that the average age at his agency, including senior management, is 28. And a PR insider tells us that most of the people in her office are her age (late 20s), and that the oldest guy in the office is 45—"but he doesn't act like it."

Depending on their agency, people in advertising and PR also tend to congregate during their nonworking hours. They go to happy hour together on Friday evenings, invite each other to parties, date, and sometimes even marry. Which means that in the bigger advertising and PR cities, if you get a job you're likely to get a social life as well.

All of this creates a looseness and sense of humor that you might not find in companies with more rigid processes or older, more conservative staffs. This might not be an absolute rule—things can be more uptight at the bigger, account-driven advertising agencies or the bigger PR agencies—but it's fairly safe to say that working in advertising or PR can be a lot more fun than working in most other industries.

One more note about culture: A lot of agencies have had to let people go in recent years—and others have had to go so far as to close one or more offices, or close up shop altogether. As a result, uncertainty about the future has begun to pervade the halls of some agencies; at those agencies, water-cooler conversation may consist as much of who-might-get-the-ax as of work or rumors about coworkers' love lives.

Travel

Travel requirements vary a great deal in advertising and PR. Account people or creatives with out-of-town clients do a fair amount of travel. They also may travel to oversee the production of ads, or as part of international PR work. Media, production, and traffic people in advertising, on the other hand, do hardly any traveling. And more junior people will generally traveling less than senior people. According to one advertising insider, "An assistant account executive might go along to client meetings, if they're local. And some might go to TV shoots. It all depends on who your manager is."

Compensation and Vacation

When it comes to handing out paychecks, the advertising industry is a lot like Dr. Jekyll and Mr. Hyde. When you first start in advertising, it's Mr. Hyde: Low to mid-$20,000s—low $30,000s at most—depending on your position and your experience. "It's not very high pay for fairly long hours," says one insider. Another says, "The young people in the business do tough jobs for not a lot of money. It's a classic case of paying your dues."

As you advance in the industry, though, you'll get to know Dr. Jekyll: into the $80,000s and $90,000s and even into the six figures if you make VP or director or are a recognized creative talent.

In PR, the numbers (and the fact that they start very small but can get fairly sizeable as you advance in your career) are quite similar.

Vacation policies are fairly standard. Most firms offer 2 weeks to start, 3 weeks after a few years; others are more liberal. And if you're a valuable asset to an agency, you can command significant vacation time. One advertising creative we spoke with takes a couple of months off—paid—to go on a big trip every 4 years or so.

Training

Training policies vary widely throughout these industries. Many advertising and PR agencies offer no formal training at all. Those that do offer training programs are generally bigger, more-established agencies. In advertising, these include Young & Rubicam, Grey Global Group, J. Walter Thompson, and Leo Burnett (which even has formal training for entry-level creatives).

In addition, lots of agencies offer internships to students. Insiders say that internships can be very valuable in helping you learn more about advertising or PR and can be impressive on your resume when it comes to landing a full-time job. But beware: Some agencies offer internships that teach you about the business, whereas other agencies use internship positions to get cheap, temporary clerical help.

Career Notes

Undergraduates

Undergraduates are the primary fodder for entry-level positions in the advertising and PR industries. Media assistant, account coordinator, production assistant—these and other positions like them in advertising are full of recent college graduates. The same thing is true of account coordinators in PR. You don't need an MBA or any other advanced degree to break in, but you can count on doing some grunt clerical and number-crunching work.

Many people get into advertising by taking purely clerical positions, generally as administrative assistants. Opinions about these jobs vary. If you start as an administrative assistant, "people don't stop looking at you as a secretary," according to one insider. But another says that her agency has an excellent record of promoting people out of administrative assistant positions. It's something to consider if you're trying to break into the business.

MBAs

Most MBAs aren't interested in advertising and PR because the entry-level salaries are not as attractive as in other industries. But because of their training in business strategies, MBAs can fit in well in account management, account planning, and media planning.

A few years back, some advertising agencies, such as Saatchi & Saatchi and Young & Rubicam, did take to hiring MBAs for account management positions. But for the most part, it's not necessary to have an MBA to get a job in advertising or PR, and the career path for MBAs will not necessarily be any better than that for undergraduate hires.

Midcareer Candidates

Midcareer professionals coming from other industries should be prepared to start at square one. Advertising and PR are industries in which people generally start at the bottom and work their way up. It's often necessary to jump from agency to agency to move ahead. Finding leads on new jobs is usually not a problem, though, since the advertising and PR communities in most regions are quite close-knit. In PR, career changers with extensive industry knowledge, government experience, or experience dealing with the press can enter at more advanced levels.

Midcareer advertising and PR people looking to jump agencies will find they're judged by the success of the campaigns they've worked on.

Insider Scoop

What Employees Really Like

Variety Show

No matter where you work in advertising or PR, you'll have the opportunity to experience quite a bit of variety as you progress in your career. You'll get to work on different accounts, each with its own problems to solve. Over time, you might work on everything from a computer software account to a sporting goods account. One advertising account management insider says, "It's never dull. You're always working on a bunch of different things. If you thrive on variety, you'll probably like advertising." An advertising creative agrees: "Your job is constantly changing. It's a dynamic job description."

"It's a party every day."

One insider swears he says just that to his wife every evening when she asks how the office was that day. Of course, he's kidding, but he likes the atmosphere. "It's light," he says. "There are a lot of young people." A creative insider says, "For a corporate environment, it's the most relaxed you can get. The dress is casual, you can joke around with people, there may be a pool table or a Ping-Pong table or that kind of thing. . . ." Another advertising creative insider agrees: "Even when I have a bad day at work, I laugh really hard several times during the day." A PR insider says, "We all go out together all the time." An advertising account management insider sums it up: "A lot of fun and interesting people work in the industry."

Hey, Good-Lookin'

Advertising is notorious for drawing in attractive young people who dress well and go to the hippest restaurants and bars. One insider says, "As much as we joke about it, there is a glamorous element to the industry. You get to stay at good hotels and go to cool restaurants and work with cool directors. The parties are just full of great-looking people." But, he adds, "Sometimes it seems a little unreal and superficial. And half the people at these parties work in traffic or write direct-response ads, so how glamorous can it really be?"

The Right-Brain Stuff

Most people in advertising like the fact that they work with a creative product, whether they're creatives or not. "You get to use one side of your brain for the business details, while using the other side for helping develop the creative work," says an account management insider. Another insider agrees: "It's really fun to be involved in creative things even if you're not creative yourself."

Changing the World

"Just Do It." "Whassup." "Don't leave home without it." In advertising and PR, you're involved in a world of high visibility and great cultural power. "At its best, you can do something that contributes to popular culture," says an insider. "You can do a spot that enters the zeitgeist." Even if the result is not as earth-shattering as that, people in advertising consider it a compelling industry. "You get to see what you've created on national TV, and advertising is a topic that everyone has an opinion about," another insider says.

PR is similar: There can be a real charge to seeing a press strategy you worked on reflected in a story in a big newspaper or magazine.

Watch Out!

Changing the World? Not!

No matter how much some people in the industry would like to believe good advertising is the same as art, the fact is it's not. "It's probably as base a consumer-oriented thing as you can do," says an insider. And though some people in the industry think advertising provides a great benefit to society, others disagree completely. One insider says, "You're not saving the world; you're not saving orphans. You're not doing much of value to mankind." Another puts it this way: "Sometimes, I think of all the smart, talented people I work with, who work really hard solving problems together all day. And I have to think there are better ways their energy could be directed, instead of selling a bunch of crap to people who don't need it." In fact, in advertising you may end up advertising a product you don't particularly think much of.

And PR's no different, in this regard. Someone's got to spin the story for the oil company after the big spill at sea; someone's got to defend the chemical company that doesn't want to pay damages to the third-world community over which its facility released a cloud of noxious gas. That someone works in PR.

Ego a-Go-Go

For some reason, advertising is an industry full of people with quirky, intrusive habits and bloated egos. (The same thing can be true in PR, though that industry's not as notorious as advertising for this.) There's the copywriter who won't go into creative presentations without his parrot perched on his shoulder. Or the creative director who sees no problem with practicing scales on his saxophone—in the office in the middle of the afternoon. Or the commercial director who calls her ads "films."

"My bosses are the most arrogant people I've ever met," says an insider. Another says, "There are a lot of difficult people in the industry. And as an account person, you have to kiss butts, and that can get frustrating." And sometimes it seems the arrogant egomaniacs are the ones who make it far in the business. One insider says, "I've never worked with so many rich idiots before."

The Client Kowtow

Advertising creatives are unanimous in occasionally disliking aspects of the agency's relationship with the client, and most people in the business have been frustrated by their dealings with clients at some point. One insider says, "We had a bagel client who insisted that we not have any punctuation in the ad copy. It was the most absurd client demand I'd ever heard." Another says, "You can spend 6 months working on a project that just suddenly dies [because the client changes its mind]." Another complains about foreign clients that don't "get it," like the Asian auto manufacturer that kills great creative ads because it doesn't understand American humor. An account management insider says, "I hate having to baby-sit the client." As another insider notes, though, "You need the client. So you have to compromise your integrity sometimes."

Dysfunctional Press Relationships

In PR, a lot of your job involves calling members of the press. Day in, day out. Problem is, many members of the press can't stand PR people and aren't afraid to let you know that. One insider says, "There are some press who'll just hang up on you, or start yelling at you." She goes on to say that the stuff she works on still ends up making its way into those press members' stories.

Capsizing Careers

As one advertising insider says, "This industry is notoriously unstable." An advertising agency might lose a big account, and suddenly 20 percent of its staff is laid off. Or a creative might find herself assigned to a partner or a creative director she can't work with and—boom!—she's fired. Or a junior account person might rub a big, important client the wrong way, and suddenly he's reassigned to the direct response unit of the agency. Note: The same kind of instability exists in PR.

Getting Hired

- The Recruiting Process

- Interviewing Tips

- Grilling Yourself

- Grilling Your Interviewer

The Recruiting Process

Many of the big advertising agencies do at least some on-campus recruiting—most commonly for account management positions, media positions, and account planning positions. Be on the lookout for firms that recruit at your school.

Generally, the first interview will take place on campus. Candidates the agency is interested in will then interview with more people at the agency's offices.

In your interviews, you'll be asked about things on your resume that show you're advertising or PR material. You'll be expected to show that you have good marketing sense, an understanding of the business of advertising and the workings of the media, and a pleasant personality. Your interviewer will also want to know why you're looking at his or her agency, so be sure to bone up on its recent work and news. And if you're going into account management (in advertising and PR), your interviewer will pay special attention to your leadership potential, so be prepared to talk about experiences in which you took on a leadership role.

Networking

Most people don't get their jobs in advertising or PR through on-campus recruiting. Most get their jobs the old-fashioned way—they network. Although responding to an online job listing or classified ad is a possibility, the best way to get in the door at an advertising or PR agency is to know somebody. One insider says point-blank, "Networking is really important in this industry. Find a friend of a friend who knows somebody in the agency you want to work for. Or read

Advertising Age and write a letter to the vice presidents who are mentioned and who work where you want to work." Another option is to go to your school's career office to see if it has a list of alumni contacts in the advertising or PR industry.

Insider Tip

Even entry-level creative job seekers need a polished, professional-looking book to land a good job.

Do not send your resume to agency HR departments. In most cases, it'll just go into the circular file.

Instead, work your contacts to get in touch with someone who can make a hiring decision or who can recommend you to someone with hiring power.

Advertising Creatives

Creatives must take a different path into advertising. For them, it's less about who they know, where they went to school, or what their grades were. Creatives must have a good book to get a job. As one insider puts it, "It's not about your resume, it's about your book."

Nowadays, even entry-level creative job seekers need a polished, professional-looking book to land a good job. Many aspiring creatives go to advertising schools, which help them hone their concepting skills while they put together a book. Among the more popular schools are the Portfolio Center, the Creative Circus in Atlanta, the University of Texas at Austin, and the Art Center in Pasadena. Other aspiring creatives take a job as an administrative assistant in a creative department where they can get to know successful creatives and get advice on putting together a good book.

Creatives also need perseverance. Good advertising is a subjective thing. To get a job, you need to get your book in front of a creative director who likes it at the same time the agency has an opening. Be prepared to hear "thanks, but no thanks" from lots of agencies. As one insider says, "I have an envelope full of rejection letters that's 3 inches thick."

Public Relations Notes

In PR, it's all about excellent communication skills. Because you'll be spending much of your day on the phone with members of the press, you've got to be a good speaker and able to think on your feet. And because you'll be writing press releases, if not speeches for client executives, you've got to be a strong writer. You'll most likely be expected to take a writing test as part of the interview process. Be forewarned.

Like advertising creatives, PR candidates can improve their opportunities by putting together a portfolio of related work. If you're already in the industry, that means press releases and press mentions for your accounts. If you're looking to break into the industry, that can mean everything from that college paper you aced, to the event flyers you created for your student organization's big charitable event, to a copy of the presentation you made to your school's administration defending your fraternity or sorority. The idea is to show the strength of your writing skills and your ability to craft a message for the audience you want to reach and to show that you can be persuasive and improve the image of organizations you're aligned with.

Interviewing Tips

1. If you've done an internship in the advertising or PR industry, talk about all that you learned from it. Internship experience gives you a step up on the competition for entry-level jobs.

2. Show that advertising or PR is where you want to be. Play up anything on your resume that has to do with marketing or creativity, and talk about how much you want to work in a business that highlights both.

3. Do your homework. Most interviewers will want to hear what you know about the industry's history and its recent trends. This will gauge how serious you are about the job. Check out other resources, listed at the end of this guide. Use your contacts to find advertising or PR professionals who will talk to you about the business and their experience in it.

4. You should also learn about the agency you're interviewing with. Visit its website, and if it's an ad agency, learn more about it in *The Red Book* and check out its ads. One insider says, "If you think the work is horrible, odds are you're going to hate the agency." Know who its current clients are and think about the strategies behind different campaigns it's working on. Be prepared to talk about why you would prefer to work at a particular agency rather than at its competitors.

5. Be specific when talking about your experiences and how they show your marketing acumen, analytical ability, and leadership skills. Don't just say, "I was the house manager of my fraternity." Instead, talk about how you rallied your fraternity brothers to keep the fraternity house clean and motivated a team of brothers to refinish the house's hardwood floors.

6. This may seem difficult, but it's important to be attentive and enthused during your interview, while seeming relaxed and at ease at the same time. Advertising and PR are all about relationships, and it'll help your chances of getting a job if you can show that you'll be easy to work with.

7. Be prepared to do some creative thinking or problem solving. You might have to talk about how you would change an existing ad or press campaign to make it more effective. Or you might have to talk about how you'd go about designing a media or press plan for a given account.

8. Don't forget the thank-you note. You never know—it might be what makes the difference between you and another candidate.

Grilling Yourself

Following are the kinds of questions you might expect in an advertising or PR interview. Be prepared for these and you'll have an easier time with the unexpected questions as well.

- What excites you most about a career in advertising/PR?

- Where do you want to end up in advertising/PR?

- What makes you want to work for this agency rather than for our competitors?

- Pretend I'm a prospective client, and you're pitching me. Explain why I should give my account to your agency.

- Tell me about your leadership experience. (This question is for account managers in both advertising and PR.)

- Tell me about a time when you were faced with a problem that was difficult to solve. What was the problem? What steps did you take to solve it? How was the situation resolved?

- Tell me about a time when you worked together with a team. What was the team trying to do? What was your role within the team? Was the team successful in achieving its goals?

- What other agencies are you interviewing with?

- Sell me this pencil.

Grilling Your Interviewer

This is your chance to turn the tables and find out what you personally want to know about advertising or PR. We strongly encourage you to come up with some questions on your own. In the meantime, the following sample questions should get you started. Rare questions are meant to be boring and innocuous, while those in the Well-Done section will help you put the fire to your interviewer's feet.

Rare

- What made you choose this agency?
- How did you get into advertising/PR?
- What's a typical career path in this department?

Medium

- For advertising account services: How much of the job consists of overseeing the execution of advertisements, and how much consists of doing strategic or competitive analysis?
- For advertising account services: Will I get to go on shoots? To client meetings?
- Is it possible to move laterally within the agency?
- Is it possible to get promoted out of an administrative assistant position?
- What are the exiting new business opportunities for the agency?

Well-Done

- What do you find most frustrating about the industry? About the agency?
- How well do the different departments of the agency get along?
- How has the consolidation of the industry affected the agency?

- If the agency has been acquired: Has the new arrangement affected the business or the culture of the agency?

- If the agency has not been acquired: Do you think the agency needs to be acquired by a bigger company to remain competitive?

- What percentage of your professional staff are women and minorities?

- What's the agency's policy regarding layoffs if you lose a big account?

For Your Reference

- Advertising and Public Relations Lingo

- Advertising Resources

- Public Relations Resources

Advertising and Public Relations Lingo

While it won't get you the job in and of itself, it certainly won't hurt you in your interviews to understand some lingo from advertising and PR. To help with this, we've compiled a list of some common advertising and PR lingo.

15, 30, 60. Different-length TV spots. As in "The client wants two 30s and a 60."

Advertorial. Print ad that has the appearance of an article or editorial in the publication in which it appears.

Backgrounder. A document that details market position, place in history, and market need met by a company or one of its product or service offerings. Often accompanies a press release about the company, product, or service.

Banner. Online advertisement of the kind typically found at the top and in the margins of a website. Potential customers click through the banner to access more extensive marketing messaging from the advertiser.

Book. A portfolio of a creative's ad samples. For aspiring copywriters and art directors, a book will consist of mock ads. For someone already in the business, it will consist of actual ads that person helped create.

Boilerplate. Standard wording that goes at the bottom of a given organization's press releases.

Boutique. An agency that focuses on only one aspect of advertising; for example, a creative boutique would handle only creative duties for a client, not media planning or research.

Brief. The creative brief, a formal memo written by account management or account planning, detailing the agency's creative strategy for an account.

Broadcast advertising. Television and radio advertising.

Bus cards. The advertising posters attached to the backs and sides of buses.

Call tree. List of people to call in the event of a crisis. A term commonly used in certain PR disciplines, crisis management not least among them.

CPM. Cost per thousand, a measure of a media plan's cost versus its reach.

Campaign. An advertising effort on behalf of a brand. Some campaigns consist of just one advertisement, while others consist of a series of ads linked by the way they address a single strategy for the brand. Also, a PR effort in support of an organization's image with the public, the government, or employees.

Comp. A near-final-quality representation of a print ad.

Cut. An edited version of a commercial. As in "The client didn't like the latest cut."

Display ad. Illustrated print ad.

Dummy. Preliminary mock-up of an ad.

Editorial. News articles, features, and op-eds in print publications.

Flighting. A media plan's scheduling of TV ads.

Frequency. A measure of how frequently an ad reaches its target audience. Along with reach, frequency gives advertisers a feel for the effectiveness of a media plan.

GRP. Gross rating points, a measure of an ad's reach among TV viewers.

Impressions. The number of times a marketing message is seen.

Influencers. Those whose opinion or coverage of a company or its products or services can shape public opinion of that company or its products or services.

Linage. A measure of the size of a print ad, based on the number of lines it takes up.

Mechanical. Final production department version of a print ad, ready to go out for final production.

Mindshare. How much "space" a product, service, organization, or message takes up in an individual or group's head or collective heads.

Network. A collection of advertising agencies all sharing resources under the same corporate umbrella.

Noise. The effect of too many messages being delivered to the marketplace simultaneously. Great ad and PR campaigns strive to be heard above the noise.

Outdoor advertising. This has nothing to do with the spate of SUV ads depicted smiling yuppies on their way to the great outdoors. It refers to outdoor locations for advertisement placement, such as billboards, kiosks, and buses.

PSA. Public service announcement. These are ads for good causes ("This is your brain. This is your brain on drugs."). Ad agencies usually do them for little compensation. They give agencies a chance to enhance their public image and do good creative work.

Piggyback. Two commercials in a row from the same TV advertiser.

Pitch. An attempt to sell the agency to the client; an attempt to win new business.

Positioning. How the market thinks of a company or product, as compared to that company or product's competitors.

Pre-pro. Preproduction meeting, a meeting that takes place before a shoot.

Proactive PR. When a PR effort causes editorial. Compare to *Reactive PR.*

Rate card. Summary of various costs for different ad sizes placements in a particular publication.

Reach. A measure of how much of its targeted audience an ad or piece of editorial containing a PR message reaches.

Reactive PR. When editorial causes a PR effort. Compare to *Proactive PR.*

Reel. A collection of a creative's TV ad samples, or a collection of a commercial director's ads, that the agency and the client will use to select a director to shoot their ad.

Reprint. Reproduction of a print ad, usually used as an entry in awards shows or in a creative's book.

Ride the boards. Go out into the field to check out outdoor ad locations.

Roadblock. When a single advertisement is scheduled such that it appears on more than one TV station at the same time.

Rough. A preliminary draft of a print ad, created as a first attempt to execute the ad's concept.

Shoot. The filming of a TV ad.

The Shows. The advertising awards shows.

Spot. TV or radio commercial.

Spot market. Local media market.

Spread. A print ad covering two facing pages in a publication.

Storyboard. A print representation of how a commercial or other filmed, videotaped, or animated piece of marketing is supposed to look when finished.

Suits. The creatives' moniker for people who work on the business side of the agency.

TRP. Targeted rating points, a measure of an ad's reach among TV viewers.

Talent. Actor or voiceover person.

Target. The people the advertiser is trying to sell to.

Tissue. Very rough expression of a creative idea, often in magic marker on tissue paper.

Advertising Resources

Advertising Awards Books

It's a good idea to look at these to see what shops are making the most exciting ads.

- *One Show Annual*
- *Commercial Arts Advertising Annual, Communication Arts magazine*
- *Art Directors' Annual, from the Art Directors Club*
- *Graphis Advertising Annual*

Industry Magazines and Other News Sources

- *Advertising Age* (www.adage.com)
- *Adweek* (www.adweek.com)
- The *New York Times* advertising column every day in the business section

Books About Advertising

The Red Book: Standard Directory of Advertising Agencies

National Register Publishing (New Providence, NJ).
Provides details on all advertising agencies. This is a great place to learn about which agencies you might be interested in.

Hey, Whipple, Squeeze This: A Guide to Creating Great Ads

Luke Sullivan (Adweek Books, 1988).
A humorous, intelligent guide to the ad game by a successful copywriter.

How to Put Your Book Together: A Guide to Creating Great Ads

Maxine Paetro and Giff Crosby (Copy Workshop, 1988).
A valuable guide for aspiring creatives.

Positioning: The Battle for Your Mind

Al Ries and Jack Trout (Warner Books, 1993).
An incisive guide to marketing effectively by communicating effectively.

Adcult USA: The Triumph of Advertising in American Culture

James B. Twitchell (Columbia University Press, 1997).
A look at the central role advertising plays in modern culture.

Soap, Sex, and Cigarettes: A Cultural History of American Advertising

Julian Sivulka (Wadsworth Publishing Co., 1997).
A study of the social and cultural importance of advertising.

The Advertising Age Encyclopedia of Advertising

John McDonough, Karen Egolf, and Jacqueline V. Reid, editors (Fitzroy
Dearborn Publishers, 2002).
Three-volume set that that takes an exhaustive look at the history of
advertising. Includes profiles of 120 important past and present agencies, an
overview of advertising tactics, profiles of top advertisers, descriptions of
seminal ad campaigns, and so on.

Encyclopedia of Major Marketing Campaigns

Thomas Riggs, editor (Gale Group, 1999).
Case studies of 500 of the most important advertising and marketing
campaigns of the 20th century, from Timex's "It Takes a Lickin' and Keeps on
Tickin'" to the California Milk Processor Board's "Got Milk?"

Truth, Lies and Advertising: The Art of Account Planning

Jon Steel (John Wiley & Sons, 1998).

All about account planning.

Other Resources

University of Texas Advertising Department

The Advertising Department at the University of Texas hosts a great site, full
of resources, information, and links. Check it out at
http://advertising.utexas.edu/world/index.asp.

"The Advertising Century" by *Advertising Age*

This feature, which looks at 20th century advertising, includes the top 100
advertising campaigns, the top ten ad icons (think: the Marlboro Man), the top
100 people in the industry, and so on. Catch it at www.adage.com/century/.

Abbott Wool's Market Segment Resource Locator

Links to a variety of ethnic ad agencies: www.awool.com.

Account Planning Group

Here, you can download "What Is Account Planning?", which details what
account planners do and what kinds of people fit well in this role. (Click on the
Downloads link in the Resources section of the site.) www.apg.org.uk.

Public Relations Resources

Industry News Sources

PR Week

The industry standard when it comes to PR news and analysis: www.prweek.com.

PRSA News

An online feed of PR news, brought to you by the Public Relations Society of America: www.prsa.org/_News/main/index.asp?ident=index1.

Books about Public Relations

The New PR Toolkit: Strategies for Successful Media Relations

Deirdre Breakenridge and Tom DeLoughry (Financial Time Prentice Hall, 2003). How-to book covers PR strategy and execution, with case studies.

PR!

Stuart Ewen (Basic Books, 1998).
A thorough social history of public relations.

Full Frontal PR:
Getting People Talking about You, Your Business, or Your Product

Richard Laermer and Michael Prichinello (Bloomberg Press, 2003).
By an industry pro, and chock full of the tricks of the trade.

The PR Crisis Bible:
How to Take Charge of the Media When All Hell Breaks Loose

Robin Cohn (Truman Talley Books, 2000).
Insight into how crisis management PR works.

The Guide to Financial Public Relations:
How to Stand Out in the Midst of Competitive Clutter

Larry Chambers (Saint Lucie Press, 1999).
Details the ins and outs of this PR specialty.

The Tipping Point: How Little Things Can Make a Big Difference

Malcolm Gladwell (Little Brown & Company, 2000).
A look at how trends start. Required reading for PR and other marketing types.

Other Resources

The Holmes Report

This organization publishes a wealth of information about PR. Included on its website are descriptions of hundreds of PR agencies. Check it out at www.holmesreport.com.

The Public Relations Society of America

News, professional development resources, networking groups, job listings. Available at www.prsa.org.

Internet PR Guide

News, career tips, and so on, at www.internetprguide.com.

The Museum of Public Relations

Learn about important individuals and milestones in PR: www.prmuseum.com.

All About Public Relations with Steven R. Van Hook

How-to articles, links to industry resources and job listings, and career information: www.aboutpublicrelations.net.

JOB SEARCH GUIDES

Getting Your Ideal Internship

Job Hunting A to Z: Landing the Job You Want

Killer Consulting Resumes

Killer Investment Banking Resumes

Killer Resumes & Cover Letters

Negotiating Your Salary & Perks

Networking Works!

INTERVIEW GUIDES

Ace Your Case: Consulting Interviews

Ace Your Case II: 15 More Consulting Cases

Ace Your Case III: Practice Makes Perfect

Ace Your Case IV: The Latest & Greatest

Ace Your Case V: Even More Practice Cases

Ace Your Interview!

Beat the Street: Investment Banking Interviews

Beat the Street II: Investment Banking Interview Practice Guide

CAREER & INDUSTRY GUIDES

Careers in Accounting

Careers in Advertising & Public Relations

Careers in Asset Management & Retail Brokerage

Careers in Biotech & Pharmaceuticals

Careers in Brand Management

Careers in Consumer Products

Careers in Entertainment & Sports

Careers in Human Resources

Careers in Information Technology

Careers in Investment Banking

Careers in Management Consulting

Careers in Manufacturing

Careers in Marketing & Market Research

Careers in Non-Profits & Government

Careers in Real Estate

Careers in Supply Chain Management

Careers in Venture Capital

Consulting for PhDs, Doctors & Lawyers

Industries & Careers for MBAs

Industries & Careers for Undergraduates

COMPANY GUIDES

Accenture

Bain & Company

Boston Consulting Group

Booz Allen Hamilton

Citigroup's Corporate & Investment Bank

Credit Suisse First Boston

Deloitte Consulting

Goldman Sachs Group

J.P. Morgan Chase & Company

Lehman Brothers

McKinsey & Company

Merrill Lynch

Morgan Stanley

25 Top Consulting Firms

Top 20 Biotechnology & Pharmaceuticals Firms

Top 25 Financial Services Firms